brilliant
presentation

How to overcome your nerves and learn the basic ways to become a brilliant presenter.

You'll learn everything – from the planning of the presentation, the building of the story, the creation of the slides, the focus on the audience, the practising of the performance and the follow up.

Presenting has never been more important.

Here's how to be brilliant at it.

B100 000000 3425 E2

PEARSON
Prentice Hall
BUSINESS

Books that make you better

Books that make you better. That make you *be* better, *do* better, *feel* better. Whether you want to upgrade your personal skills or change your job, whether you want to improve your managerial style, become a more powerful communicator or be stimulated and inspired as you work.

Prentice Hall Business is leading the field with a new breed of skills, careers and development books. Books that are a cut above the mainstream – in topic, content and delivery – with an edge and verve that will make you better, with less effort.

Books that are as sharp and smart as you are.

Prentice Hall Business.
We work harder – so you don't have to.

For more details on products, and to contact us, visit
www.pearsoned.co.uk

brilliant
presentation

What the best presenters know,
say and do

Richard Hall

Harlow, England • London • New York • Boston • San Francisco • Toronto
Sydney • Tokyo • Singapore • Hong Kong • Seoul • Taipei • New Delhi
Cape Town • Madrid • Mexico City • Amsterdam • Munich • Paris • Milan

PEARSON EDUCATION LIMITED

Edinburgh Gate
Harlow CM20 2JE
Tel: +44 (0)1279 623623
Fax: +44 (0)1279 431059
Website: www.pearsoned.co.uk

First published in Great Britain in 2007

© Pearson Education Limited 2007

ISBN: 978-0-273-70974-9

British Library Cataloguing-in-Publication Data
A catalogue record for this book is available from the British Library

Library of Congress Cataloging-in-Publication Data
A catalog record for this book is available from the Library of Congress

10 9 8 7 6 5 4 3 2 1
11 10 09 08 07

Typeset in 10/14pt Latin 725 by 3
Printed and bound in Great Britain by Ashford Colour Press Ltd., Gosport, Hants.

The publisher's policy is to use paper manufactured from sustainable forests.

Contents

Acknowledgements   ix

Introduction   xi

1   The stuff of brilliant presentations   1
Fires   1
The five critical processes   3

2   Coping with nerves   5
Nerves are normal   5
It's the voice that is key   5
How to avoid freezing   6
So how do accomplished presenters feel?   7
Be honest with yourself   7
What is actually going on?   8
Be self-aware   9
To be nervous is normal   10
Scary but nice   14

3   The five levels of mastery   15
The world of the non-presenter   15
Level one – novice presenter   16
Level two – apprentice presenter   17
Level three – craftsman presenter   18
Level four – star presenter   20
Level five – brilliant presenter   21

4   The context of the presentation   23
Have you got the plot?   23
First of all get the exam question right   23

5   How to write a great story 31
     A great story 31
     Death to mission statements and other jargon 31
     The truth is a powerful weapon 33
     Does the story grab the imagination? 34
     Become a story student 35
     The best presentations were great stories 35
     Great memory hook but what's the story? 36
     What a story! 37

6   How to give your story colour 39
     A nearly great presentation in the making 39
     A bare presentation is like bare walls 40

7   How to illustrate your presentation 47
     Think of slides as your music 47
     Bad slides slow you down 47
     Professional slides make a presentation sing 48
     Professorial vagueness has its place 48
     Less is more 49
     Why people avoid slides 53
     Are you ever allowed to be boring? 55

8   Performance 57
     What acting can do 57
     In praise of work – in praise of America 57
     Illogical arguments show up in a presentation 58
     Why? Why?? Why??? Why???? Why????? 60
     A strong argument helps you feel confident in performance 60
     A little bit of theatricality is vital on stage 66

9   I've got the power 67
     PowerPoint 67

Be fair – blame the workman not his tools   68

PowerPoint has improved lives   69

Let's get a bit more technical   70

Things to do to your PC   71

One chance and only one   74

You thought the technical stuff was easy?   75

10   This book as a presentation   79

Following my own advice ... almost   79

Discovering what really happens   79

How to do brilliant presentations   80

11   Really understanding your audience   99

What's up?   99

Lessons about how to understand audiences   100

12   From ordinary to brilliant   105

A change and a commitment   105

Getting the story right will drive everything else   106

How do the superstars do it?   106

13   The graduation to brilliance   115

A scale of improvement   115

14   So you made it   127

This is a formula   127

How with it are you?   128

Presentation has never been more important   128

Brilliance will be achieved if ...   130

Acknowledgements

I'd like to thank my wife Kate for her help and patience in tolerating my occasional irritation and for making consistently significant suggestions.

Thanks to Pearson and Rachael Stock and Samantha Jackson for their efforts. I'd particularly like to congratulate Rachael who gave birth to twins while I was writing this.

Most of all I'd like to acknowledge all the great presenters and actors I've seen – people who can make a presentation fly and take fire. It is from them that the inspiration in this book really came.

Brilliant presenters are rare. Watch out for them and study them.

Introduction

This is about what it takes to be a *brilliant presenter*, how much work you will have to do and why it matters. Being a good presenter has never been more important. Being a brilliant presenter can transform your career.

Why it matters

In an information economy the ability to convey facts and argument clearly may be the most valuable skill of all.
    Thomas Weber: Stanford University, USA.

Bad presentation is tantamount to fraud.
    The Financial Times

It isn't easy

Being a brilliant anything isn't easy. You need some talent, a huge desire to get better, a practical tool kit, a great deal of practice and a lot of hard work and discipline. Being a brilliant presenter is not easy – unless you have the tools to do it, which this book gives you.

Here is the basic tool kit, some critical pointers and much encouragement. Read it and apply it and I guarantee that you will be a good, if not brilliant, presenter in a few months – *provided* that you are prepared to be honest about where you stand in the presenters' league table now; and *provided* that you are prepared to put in the hours of practice and homework you will need if you are to move up that table. It should also make you feel a little more relaxed about your quest for excellence when you realise that you are starting at the bottom of the league in very good company.

You have to learn the art and craft

It has always astounded me that so many companies and so many executives assume that presentation is an innate gift, like walking or running or swimming. Swimming? Take anyone and throw them in the deep end and watch them swim ... or, more likely, drown. Like swimming, presenting is something you *learn*. Some people are naturally good at it and think nothing of standing up in front of a room of people and talking to them. If you are one of those lucky few you *still* need to read this book because then you might, just might, become a brilliant presenter – a gold medal orator. However, most will flail desperately, swallow water, go blue in the face, panic and drown.

The very word 'presentation' strikes fear

All you have to do is walk into a room and shout 'presentation time' to reduce half the people there to quivering wrecks. One person I coached found it seriously hard to remember his own name and what his job was when made to stand up in a room empty of people apart from me. I could even see his legs shaking – sudden and unexpected death would have been preferable to this torture.

Frightened or feeble – take your pick

So we have two key issues which impede a great, or even simply a competent, presentation being delivered:

- nerves so bad that they create what I call 'panic drowners';
- a lack of knowledge as to what to do (and this breed is very common) – I call these 'non-swimmers'.

Rob Harper, a leading UK swimming coach based in Finchley, told me smilingly that there is a third category of people – he calls them 'silent drowners' – who simply and miserably take in a lot of water and sink without trace.

There are quite a few presenters like that too.

What can happen if you can't do presentation

So does presenting matter? The ex-CEO of Rentokil memorably said, after a particularly heavily criticised presentation to analysts a few years ago, 'I'm paid to be a CEO not an actor'. Shortly afterwards, in consequence of the analysts' reactions to his presentation, he was fired.

We are, all of us, exposed daily to very competent presentations by people called newsreaders and anchormen on chat shows. We have a benchmark. It is no longer acceptable to appear nervous or shifty or lost for words. We must not be what high court judges sometimes call 'unreliable witnesses.'

The so-called 'transparency' of contemporary life means that managers and CEOs are simply asked more and more questions. Their ability to stand up and talk fluently about almost anything and, more importantly, to stand up for their company with clarity and command is the least we expect. Good presentations equate to money – more of it – for you and the shareholders.

So, in reality, competent presentation matters a lot. Investors in companies take a lot of notice of the confidence and conviction with which a leader talks about a company and its plans. How else, they argue, can they tell what the real prospects are? If the CEO is uncertain about what is going on, or if it seems as though they are probably being spun a lie, why on earth should they put that precious pension money at risk in that company's care? A senior analyst told me that he wanted 'to see the whites of their eyes'. In saying this he represented the confrontational nature of the analyst–executive relationship fairly. But he also wanted to see his investment on its feet and sweating.

Presentation in everyday life

Jeremy Paxman, in contrast, doesn't need to look into any politicians' eyes – he starts from the assumption that 'they're lying to me – it's up to me to find out about what'.

And if presentation does have a slightly dodgy reputation it's because people like Peter Mandelson, Alistair Campbell and Philip Gould – the architects of New Labour – created a new level of aggressive spin which, while enormously effective at framing agendas and putting opponents on the back foot, makes many people uncertain of what is true and what is not, and forces many of us to presume that all politicians are probably guilty of mendacious behaviour.

The 'must haves' in business today

Away from the increasingly murky and spinning-a-line world of politics, however, there's a shortlist of must-haves if you want to get on in life. Here it is:

- Can (and do) you read?
- Can (and do) you write?
- Can you add up?
- Can you think (on your feet)?
- Can you perform simple tasks consistently well?
- Can you show initiative?
- Can you do what you are told?
- Can you present brilliantly?

Nowadays presenting is taught as a routine skill in many schools. I wish that we non-swimmers/non-presenters had been so lucky.

Presentations are normal for all of us now

At almost every level of every company the need to do a presentation of some sort occurs quite often. This could be a simple speech of thanks – that's a presentation; or a description of the activities of your department to a visitor – that's a presentation too; or the story about the new marketing campaign accompanied by visual aids and music – that is a *big* presentation.

Regard this book, at its lowest level of use, as an insurance policy. Buy it, read it and when the call to present comes you'll be fine – provided that you have followed its advice. But if you aspire to being the person who is constantly asked to present stuff because you are so good at it that people describe you as 'brilliant' then read, mark, learn and inwardly digest what's in here – then practice like mad. I have sought to make it simple, easy to read and practical.

You cannot get to be brilliant on day one

Most of all, I recognise that there are different levels of competence. I do not follow the school of advice that makes bold assumptions – such as the cookery book I read that said 'Fillet your Dover sole then cover it in flour . . .' Hang on! 'Fillet?' – how do you do that?

We are going to go through this step by step starting at the beginning. But even if you are a pretty competent performer already then what's contained here will make you better. And if you follow the advice you will improve pretty rapidly to the levels you've dreamed of.

If you want to be *brilliant* you will have to work at it. The journey starts here.

1 The stuff of brilliant presentations

What, in simple terms, is a 'brilliant presentation'? If you have only five minutes to get your act together then read this. It tells you how to achieve radical improvements. This is what they call the 'executive summary'.

Fires

How do you actually do a 'brilliant presentation' – once you have controlled your nerves? (Study Chapter 2 now for advice on this). I've talked to people who worked to templates, who recycled old presentations, who scoured *Old Bloaters' Book of Favourite Jokes and One Liners*, and I have to say I always thought it showed.

Write these five words on the wall.

**FRESH   INFORMATIVE   RELEVANT
ENTHUSIASTIC   STORY**

If you like acronyms, call this the FIRES approach. If you don't then just *think* about these five words. Whatever else you do, you just have to be able to put a tick next to each one when you've got your next presentation ready.

- **Fresh** – whatever else you do, make your material sound new, original and fresh. Try to find a couple of interesting insights. Gigantic facts can help, for instance 'All the beans Heinz sell every year would fill Wembley Stadium up to row N' sounds better than some tonnage figure. Most of all, in saying 'fresh' I'm demanding an attitude of mind that leads to every show being seen as a new show and every audience being regarded as a new audience.

- **Informative** – there are many occasions (such as in a wedding speech) when good natured entertainment is the limit of most people's ambitions. But in a business environment any presentation which doesn't provide new information, or new interpretation of existing information, isn't doing its job. Our job in business is to change things and move them on. There'll be a lot to read about the power of clear and powerful delivery and dramatic slides but, when it comes to the crunch, content is what makes the difference, not spin.

> ANY PRESENTATION WHICH DOESN'T PROVIDE NEW INFORMATION ISN'T DOING ITS JOB

- **Relevant** – don't give a presentation that is not relevant to the audience or to the circumstances in which they and the company currently find themselves. Examine what you are going to say with utter ruthlessness. Keep on asking 'is this relevant?' – if it isn't then bin it.

- **Enthusiastic** – the word 'passion' is currently (in my view) overused in business because it makes people who should know better behave with inappropriate zeal and with excessively evangelical language. This is not a church outing. This is a business. We are selling cough drops or whatever, we are not selling salvation. But we should enjoy what we do. It makes us better company. Being enthusiastic is more appealing to an audience. It also improves the pace and vitality of communication.

- **Story** – we can argue that there are many different types of presentation, but really there is only one – the one that tells a story with a beginning, a middle and an end. The context in which that story is told will vary, as will the audience and their expectations, but without a story to tell you shouldn't be presenting at all. I chair a charity organisation and I have banned the use of 'mission statement' and had it replaced by the simpler 'our story'.

It's easier to spin a mission statement (in corporate speak) than it is to spin a story because stories are told to seven-year-olds and they won't put up with nonsense and prevarication.

What we now need is a very prescriptive set of actions to perform in creating our 'brilliant presentation'.

The five critical processes

There are five key headings that you have to follow. Do what you will – stop reading the book, throw it out of the window, burn it, eat it – but whatever else you do, please do these five things.

1. Decide very clearly the *context* of your presentation.

2. Get your *key story* down to a cryptic message.

3. Develop facts around your story which give it *colour*.

4. Illustrate your story with brilliant *visuals* – or use none at all.

5. *Perform* your presentation with power and pace.

A few days ago I watched a presenter guiding a presentation along a path to a soggy mess and I wondered why his huge multinational employer hadn't recognised that presenting is a key skill in his job. Why didn't they teach the poor executive how to swim? Presenting a story or argument to an audience is a learned skill and not an innate gift for 90% of people. But it's a really important one.

> PRESENTING A STORY TO AN AUDIENCE IS A LEARNED SKILL AND NOT AN INNATE GIFT

Jack Welch, the brilliant and now retired CEO of the American company GE, as ever got it more right than most when he said 'I always thought that chart-making clarified my thinking better than anything else. Reducing a complex problem to a simple chart excited the hell out of me.'

2 Coping with nerves

Controlling your nerves (if you have them, and nearly everyone does) is the biggest step you can make towards being good at and enjoying presenting. To control them you must understand them and realise that nerves are normal. You must also realise that controlling them is a 'must do' for anyone who aspires to brilliance.

Nerves are normal

I am putting this subject right up front because to many people the whole business of doing a presentation, or indeed any solo perform-ance in front of an audience, causes physical anguish so great that it is disabling.

The ex-CEO of a major multinational confided to me that he'd cried himself to sleep following an inaugural speech he'd made at his new company – ruined by his faltering and then stuttering and drying up. He said that he'd felt like a high performance Italian car running out of fuel on a motorway.

There is little point in talking about the finer points of presenting if the prospective presenter or victim (because this is how they feel) wants to get it over and done with before bursting into tears or worse.

It's the voice that is key

In Julie Stanford's excellent compendium *The Essential Business Guide*, Chris Davidson gives some great advice. He notes that 'the voice is an excellent barometer of the body's overall level of nervousness'. He recommends the following:

- holding good posture
- breathing from the diaphragm
- keeping the voice well lubricated with water
- doing a warm-up – especially making '...ng' sounds as in 'bring' or 'bang'
- pronouncing whole words
- relaxing the face and shoulders.

This is great stuff and I endorse it – especially that advice on posture and relaxation.

How to avoid freezing

The voice coach Valentine Palmer also focuses on confidence. He talks about 'freezing', 'losing your way', 'your voice letting you down at a crucial moment'.

A presenter freezing is like an actor drying or a golfer with the yips – they lead to a large and malevolent fate. It is not something that anyone who has conquered it wants to talk about because, like blushing, it is hopefully a thing of the past.

You avoid freezing by keeping light on your feet, moving around and telling yourself 'this will be OK'. Cars don't freeze up until the oil runs out. Keeping talking to yourself is the equivalent of lubrication. You avoid losing your way by ensuring that you keep signposts and a roadmap in front of you – your script or notes will do that.

Your voice is your best friend or your worst enemy. Make sure that you water it on stage – frequently. If it seems about to give up in a croak say something like 'after too much talking recently my voice is beginning to give in ... I, however, am not'.

> YOUR VOICE IS YOUR BEST FRIEND OR YOUR WORST ENEMY

I want to dwell on this issue of nerves at some length because so long as you feel a 'confidence crisis' you will find presenting hard. You may survive an encounter with a presentation if you are very, very nervous but it is unlikely that you'll ever get beyond being graded as 'quite good' until you are in command of yourself and, especially, until you are in command of your voice.

There are exceptions of course. Arthur Rubinstein used to be sick before going on stage to play the piano ... and he had to be pushed reluctantly on. Then he played the piano and he was wonderful! Many great actors are quivering wrecks before a performance.

So how do accomplished presenters feel?

To be sure there may be a tingle or two and a rush of adrenalin but none of that wild-eyed, dry-mouthed croaking and freezing that has blighted so many careers.

However, I know of no brilliant presenter who cannot take a deep breath and, using any or all of the techniques I'll describe, not be in a state of self-control before a performance and *enjoy* it.

I heard of one female executive who lost it so badly that she froze and stared manically at the bemused audience before screaming 'Stop it! Stop it! Just stop looking at me like that ...' before rushing off. Poor thing – she had acute 'presentationitis' which, while not life threatening, is definitely career threatening and very, very nasty. So how do we cure this?

Be honest with yourself

You have to start by being totally honest with yourself and others.

■ How bad is your problem? Write it down now in detail.

■ Describe how really awful you feel when it's at its worst.

■ What is the worst it's ever been? No, confess to really the absolute worst.

- Analyse how you felt – top to toe and top to bottom.
  - how was your mouth?
  - how was your voice?
  - how were your knees?
  - how was your face?
  - could you see clearly?
  - how was your stomach?
  - how was your head?
- How did you feel about the situation you were in?

Just facing up to all this will make a huge difference to you and stop you hiding from the problem.

What is actually going on?

These acute attacks of nerves have been described and analysed in great detail by squads of experts. Successful treatment is very much the norm, although left untreated such attacks can lead eventually to agoraphobia which is much more serious.

The symptoms include shaking, a racing heart, sweating, difficulty catching breath, chest pain, dizziness, tingling in the hands and nausea, or more extremely (according to *The Analyst*) a palpable, screaming fear rising inside you.

Attacks are more frequent in winter than summer and more common in women than men. Common indications include increased blood pH levels, which is suggestive of hyperventilation. Apparently breathing more slowly (see elsewhere) or breathing into a paper bag can restore normal pH levels.

What actually happens? The brain has a small structure called the amygdala which can act like an 'anxiety switch' that flips on only when anxiety seems necessary – when you face a tiger, a raging torrent or the prospect of a presentation. No I'm not joking – presentations are one of the commonest reasons for the switch being turned on. When it is turned on adrenaline and serotonin are released making the body – going back to our primate beginnings – ready for escape. Adrenaline is also known as the 'fight or flight' hormone. It speeds everything up – the heart beats faster and blood is redirected to the muscles making you better able to fight or run away. In addition, the brain shuts down – in a life or death crisis you need instinct not brains. The problem is that the reverse is desirable during a presentation – you need your brain to work for you.

Serotonin is much more complex and in the most extreme situations can kill you. Think of the effect of magic mushrooms and you'll get the idea. It passes around your system very efficiently and quickly creating euphoria, over-reaction of the reflexes and a happy drunken state. If you are lucky this makes you feel ready to take on the world, but if you are unlucky it can make you feel as though you are about to die of a heart attack.

So now we sort of know what is going on let's do something about it.

Be self-aware

I am neither a doctor nor psychiatrist but having done hundreds of presentations I know that the most powerful tool that you have in preparing for a presentation is self-awareness. If you were flying a plane you'd do a very thorough preflight check, a routine in which you check if everything is working properly. And it is a routine – an unfailing do-it-in-this-order-every-time routine. This is what *you* must do before you present.

> THE MOST POWERFUL TOOL THAT YOU HAVE IN PREPARING FOR A PRESEN- TATION IS SELF-AWARENESS

There are a few exercises that may help you, but the chances are you will benefit from working with a professional presentation coach – especially if you are really suffering from anticipatory nerves to the point of feeling unwell.

Do you find that prospect humiliating? Well I guess you did have driving lessons? Yes? Well presenting is much more dangerous than driving.

To be nervous is normal

The body has the most brilliant defence and drug drip-feed system imaginable. You just need to understand what is going on to help to manage the effects and control them.

Everyone gets nervous. Actually that's not entirely true. Some people *claim* to be nerve free and, surprise, they are nearly always hopeless presenters – overbearing, too loud and self-obsessed.

Feeling nervous is good – used properly nerves are our 'presentation muscles'. Flexing them gives us a 'hyperperformance' feel which takes us from an ordinary to an extraordinary level of audience control.

The line to be drawn is between:

- 'acutely self-aware and ready to rock' – this is good;
- 'shivering with apprehension and wanting to go to the loo' – this is bad.

So how do you get to the first state of grace and avoid the second?

Ten top ways of helping to control your nerves

1. **Practice breathing in and out** – big breath in, count to four; then breath out, count to eight. Repeat this four times. Critically the breaths out are twice as intense as those in.

2. **Sing your nerves away** — anyone who has been unfortunate enough to have had a stutter knows only too well that this affliction happens when talking and never when singing. Try going into to your bathroom and belting out a big song, or your presentation message to some kind of rap beat.

3. **Externalise** – this was the single trick that got me off the 'if-there-was-only-a-hole-to swallow-me-up' feeling. I did a little con trick on myself and said 'imagine I could fly out of myself'. So I did a little psychological flight up into the roof beams and looked down at myself. Watching me down there put everything into perspective. I felt quite cheerful – and I performed well.

4. **Feel comfortable** – if you feel good you will generally do well. You simply feel in charge of yourself and those around you. Ronald Reagan may have been just a 'B' actor but he was an undoubted 'A*' when it came to confidence. It was said of Ronald that 'he felt comfortable in his shoes'. Next time you present, make sure you wear your comfiest shoes – and I do mean your comfiest and not your smartest.

5. **Practise in the nude** – David Heslop is the ex-CEO at Mazda and Expotel and this is his idea. The idea is that you get a full length mirror, strip naked and practise your presentation in front of it. Now David is really quite a large man but that merely adds weight to his argument that if you can do something as embarrassing as this with a straight face then a full auditorium will be nothing in comparison.

6. **Think about your audience** – the certain knowledge of what the audience might think about you may shape your content, your delivery and certainly your confidence. Try this exercise. Imagine that you have to go into two separate rooms – a blue room and a red room. You have a presentation to deliver entitled 'How I learned to become a confident presenter'.

   ■ In the blue room is an audience comprising the most intimidating teachers from school and also your current and all (yes *all*) your previous bosses, and anyone else in your life who has intimidated you.

▶

- In the red room is an audience of relatively well-behaved eleven-year-olds whom you don't know, but you do know that they have been told that you are a nice person. Now I want you to work out exactly how and why your performance will be different in front of the two audiences and why the eleven-year-olds may see you differently from the historic ogres. The difference in *your* feeling from each audience may help unlock your inbuilt 'confidence machine'.

7. **Preparation creates the confidence of the professional presenter** – when you watch a brilliant presenter at work and wonder how he does it, you need to remember that he has probably worked much harder at putting it all together than you could imagine. As a rule of thumb assume you are a senior manager planning an important presentation:

- the initial writing should take about 3 hours;

- the refinements about the same 3 hours;

- your stage one slide construction 2 hours;

- examining the slides you have had done professionally (it's worth it) 2 hours;

- the rehearsals and rewrites another 3 hours;

- going back to the drawing board and consulting with colleagues 3 hours;

- coaching on performance 3 hours.

Does 19 hours seem too long? It isn't – ask a professional. What all this preparation does is enhance your confidence and your chances of success hugely.

8. **Don't drink before you present** – I'm told a 'shot of vodka' is the answer. It isn't. Don't do it – ever. Any more than you'd expect your

surgeon to drink ('just to steady my hands') before an operation. While it might seem the answer for this particular presentation, in your stoned state you won't learn why what went well went well, and why what didn't didn't. Remember 'Lucky Jim' where Jim got horrendously drunk before a major presentation? Never, ever do it.

9. **Lying down and other exercises** – if you get those dreadful 'Why am I doing this?' 'May the world swallow me up' feelings do the following:

- slow down;
- breathe deeply, 4–8–4–8;
- lie down . . . this can really help;
- practise lip manoeuvres to loosen your mouth muscles;
- visualise yourself on form and doing well;
- lie down again – close your eyes and breathe like you've never breathed before;
- do voice exercises to get your vocal chords working;
- make sure your mouth and lips are moist.

10. **You are not going to die** – Lucy Kellaway wrote about cycling to work in the *Financial Times* on July 3rd 2006, 'Despite the risk I hardly ever feel frightened on my bike. I feel alert and alive but not scared. Recently I was cycling out one hot evening to give a speech to some business people. I was feeling fine about the ride but not about the impending talk. On the way I was nearly hit by a passenger door being flung open, I swerved and narrowly avoided a van. I put the thought to myself "how come I'm not frightened of being crushed to death but I'm terrified of minor humiliation in front of a small audience of civilised people". Suddenly I wasn't frightened any more. On the stage sweaty palms are no longer a problem.'

Everyone has nerves. The best, or at any rate the most pragmatic, among us controls them and uses them. Be pragmatic whatever else – the luckiest enjoy their nerves. Like Frank Skinner enjoys a really hot curry. A bit uncomfortable, but boy, doesn't it make you aware of your own body and your own mortality.

Scary but nice

Once conquered, those very nerves that disabled your earlier performances can turn you from novice to master. Controlling those nerves and using the tips above will help you learn how to do astonishing and exciting stuff. Recognise that skating brilliantly involves the prospect of falling (and remember falling isn't failing).

Presenting is high octane dangerous – so you are right to be nervous anyway. But do it well and the post-presentational euphoria is a great sensation. How dangerous? Here's what Stephen Spielberg said about it: 'We had snakes in *The Raiders of the Lost Ark*, bugs in *Indiana Jones and the Temple of Doom*. But supposedly man's greatest fear is public speaking. That'll be in our next picture.'

We're still waiting Stephen. It'll make *Psycho* look like *Mary Poppins*.

3 The five levels of mastery

This chapter describes the five levels you can achieve as a presenter – as you will see, most people don't get beyond level one. The whole point here is that it's hard to be competent let alone good and very hard to be brilliant. The key is to be honest about where you think you are starting on this journey of improvement.

This is not an easy journey. You can't suddenly leap up and proclaim 'I want to be a film star' and be one. It will require work, practice, effort and a lot of blood, sweat and tears – forget the blood, sweat and tears will do.

First of all let's describe the stages on the journey.

The world of the non-presenter

Before we talk about the levels of mastery themselves, we have to agree there are those who never have and feel that they never could deliver a presentation. These probably represent more than 50% of the population. This is nothing to be ashamed of, nor is it something to worry about.

Even if you are one of these, something will happen to you once you've taken the book's advice on how to draft and deliver a simple presentation. About half of you will still hate it and find it nerve-racking, but don't worry because you *will* grow to enjoy it. The other half will get bitten by the presentation bug. You'll experience the serious sense of power as you control a room of people and focus on working an audience. You will scarcely be able to wait before your next presentation or speech. You have entered that most dangerous of phases called 'new' – as in new driver, new golfer, new jogger. You are likely to sweep all before you, terrify passers-by and be alternately full and devoid of confidence. Your body will become full of adrenaline, serotonin and nerves.

> YOU'LL EXPERIENCE THE SERIOUS SENSE OF POWER AS YOU CONTROL A ROOM OF PEOPLE AND FOCUS ON WORKING AN AUDIENCE

But if you want to progress, here are the steps you need to take and a description of what reaching each level requires.

Level one – novice presenter

Surprisingly few people make it beyond this point. I call them 'weekend presenters' – people who do the odd presentation and can cope perfectly competently with small groups. They are good at their job, be it junior brand manager, HR executive or management accountant. Presentations are neither very important to them nor are they especially nervous at the prospect of addressing a breakout group.

They tend to 'busk it' and a few hours before their presentation do their own PowerPoint slides crammed with bullet points – 'a script on the screen' there to help the presenter not the audience. They make a virtue out of the low key provision of information. At all costs they avoid the risk of what I call 'theatrical performance' because this increases the potential for greater failure.

If they are asked if they want lights, make-up, autocue and a sound system, or if they are told that they'll be talking to an audience of 100, or that this can be career-shaping then the nerves will probably start to kick in.

It's important to recognise that these people are probably pretty good communicators with their peers. But they'd much rather communicate with them in small and relatively informal groups – sitting down rather than standing up.

It's also important that we don't criticise them for achieving only level one. It's a rule of this book, and life, that you need to try to get better but that it is far better being a brilliant presenter at this level than a neurotic at level two.

However, there are things they can think about if they are going to improve:

- how to declutter their slides so they are clearer and simpler for the audience to interact with;
- how to discard slides if the presentation is to a small group;
- how to give the presentation a splash of colour;
- how to think about what exactly it is they want to achieve – outcomes not just inputs;
- how to think about the audience and not themself.

What level one presenters should do now (you may be beginning to feel that you fall into this category by now) is review their last three presentations to see if they made sense, whether they could have been better, how they'd do them differently/better, and how they would cope if they were now asked to do a big presentation to senior management at a major offsite conference.

They may survive perfectly well as a novice but stepping up to the next level won't harm their career prospects.

Level two – apprentice presenter

Getting to the level of apprentice presenter is, in golfing terms, the equivalent of playing off 18 and regularly breaking 90. In cooking terms it's equivalent to being able to do anything that Jamie Oliver throws at you – dinner parties hold no terrors.

Apprentice presenters are competent. They know how to put half-decent slides and a well-argued story together. They suffer from nerves but remain in control. They've probably done about ten presentations, of which about half have been at all-singing, all-dancing sales events and audiences have been quite generous in their praise.

They realise they should have spent more time on preparation, but they are really very busy people and the thing that gets left till last is always the presentation. They know that their slides are a bit dull, but last time out they decided to build in a more visual approach but when the slide showing an herd of gazelle bolting across a plain came up they couldn't remember what it was supposed to signify – so they said 'these deer are frightened just like our competitors'. This got a laugh but made little sense when the next slide that came up said 'the competitive threat – why we should worry'.

Level two presenters are ambitious and realise that their prospects can be enhanced by being a bit more adept. There are several things they need to think about.

- Spending a lot more time on preparation.

- Going for a visual approach but with a verbal clue – 'Victim or predator?' on the gazelle slide might have helped the flow – and they *are* gazelle *not* deer, that was careless.

- Scripting themselves more tightly, especially as they move to more staged events.

- Working on the beginning, the end and the killer central slide if they are to graduate to the next level.

- They probably need to lighten up a little.

Level three – craftsman presenter

At this level their presentation skills will dramatically affect their progress. They will be asked to give speeches at events, and others will be glad to know that they are speaking at a conference.

It is widely recognised that they are confident and competent, and that they are completely reliable. They are courteous to technicians and they deliver stylish well-thought out presentations which reflect how much time, effort and creativity has been spent. In fact, they now spend a huge amount of time preparing – probably an increasing amount for each presentation they do. They keep a 'presentation box' at home into which interesting cuttings, pictures or cartoons go. They have a book of great quotations. They have become a management book junky.

Craftsmen presenters promote themselves as industry experts with a view to being candidates for invitation to international events – *What's New 2002?* in Las Vegas, a think-in for senior managers; *The Innovation Forum* in St. Lucia 2004; *New Wave Thinking in the New World* in Shanghai 2006; *Why Dubai?* 2007; *After Tom Peters … reframing the work of a player* in Buenos Aires 2008; *New Frontiers, new thinking ladders* in Sydney 2009. Their speeches have been assembled in a short book by Prentice Hall entitled *The Craft of Originality* – these craftsmen's reputations are made.

But they are still only level three craftsmen. If they were to see this rating they'd probably say, somewhat indignantly, 'but everyone says I am brilliant'. Maybe, but sometimes a bit dull, perhaps a bit second-hand. A bit – no, not just a bit – *much* too safe, too solidly in their comfort zone. They're very good but they aren't great.

They no longer get a flutter of nerves when they present. They are in perfect control. They are urbane, funny, supremely confident and consistent. They too have several things they could address to reach the next level.

■ Carry on presenting – they like doing it and the audience seems to like them.

■ Ask themselves a searching question – what are they achieving?

■ Reflect on whether or not their company – who is subsidising their activities – deserves a bigger shout in what messages are being put out. Are they selling the company hard enough? Or are they selling *themselves*?

■ Try to be more exciting, frightening, dramatic – anything to get themselves out of the safety box they are currently in.

■ Work with others to raise their game – if they were golfers we'd be wanting to get them down to low single figures.

■ Try to do one controversial and challenging presentation which puts them under a bit of pressure.

Level four – star presenter

This is the most dangerous level of all. At their very best they are Oscar winners and incomparably talented – at their worst they are just dreadful. They suffer agonies as though their stomachs were being eaten alive by nerve-fuelled ferrets before any performance. They are horrible to everyone around them before they perform – technicians, friends, colleagues, lovers, wives – everyone. They want to change everything at the very last minute – always.

Star presenters give 'prima donna' new meaning. They are supremely confident or utterly devoid of confidence. They are a mess of extremes – happy, sad, energetic, inert, loving, vindictive, inclusive, divisive. They are very focused on what they want. They have a very short attention span. They have blasts of huge creativity and then get stuck for days. They cry in private and sometimes in public too. They consistently feel sorry for themselves. Their emotional age is seven. They are often CEOs.

What they are blessed with is the rare and magic gift of being able to communicate a vision or personal dream in a language which resonates with the audience. They use beautifully simple language and short sentences – really short.

> THE RARE AND MAGIC GIFT OF BEING ABLE TO COMMUNICATE A VISION IN A LANGUAGE WHICH RESONATES WITH THE AUDIENCE

Level four presenters work with the best slide artists – those who can make a dull graph jive, who can animate the description of an operational process to make people's mouths fall open in comprehension, who make audiences want to look at that screen just to enjoy the spectacle of vivid logic unfolding before them.

Level four presenters are presentational professionals and human relations amateurs – brilliant but impossible. The reason they don't quite make level five is their selfishness and erratic behaviour. If you see yourself in this characterisation I have two things to say – congratulations, you clearly have huge talent. Now do the following if you want to become truly and consistently brilliant.

- Calm down.
- Learn the tone of voice and look that you want to project and take it from there – the late Sir Laurence Olivier used to say once he had got the walk and the clothes right everything else followed.
- Learn consistency – it will give you a longer life and earn you more friends.
- Use the most important words in management, 'thank you' and 'well done', more often. The team around you can help to lift your game on your off days and to make you fly on your good days. They need to be appreciated.
- Think more about your audience than you currently do.
- Stop showing off so much.
- Control your nerves – you might only be great by the skin of your teeth – that sounds like fragile success.

Level five – brilliant presenter

Congratulations! Join a cadre of the elite – Bill Clinton, Tim Bell, Tony O'Reilly, Alan Parker, Tom Peters, Richard Eyres, Michael Mayne, Charles Handy, Michael Portillo – and, currently, few others.

The idea, of course, is that books like this which are dedicated to the improvement of presentation skills will make 'brilliance' a less unattainable peak. In 1953 Everest was scaled for the first time – in May 2006 nearly 200 people climbed it.

Like 'flu, brilliance is catching. I define brilliance in presentation as comprising four key elements:

- deep, transcendental knowledge;
- all-consuming passion for the subject;
- the ability to tell a story in simple language;

- the theatrical ability to make a story fresh and full of a sense of discovery.

It's asking a lot of the brilliant presenter that they always be brilliant but once they've set the standard we should expect no less of them. And sometimes a star, or even craftsman, presenter can attain brilliance. Take Melvyn Bragg (a good craftsman I thought) – I saw him on stage in Brighton talking about his book *Twelve Books that Changed the World*. He was a revelation, fizzing with enthusiasm and boyish excitement. He was hopelessly lacking in discipline and ran over time, but he spoke from the depths of knowledge and discovery that drive him as a person. It was like hearing Eric Clapton playing a long improvised riff – totally brilliant.

I asked Will Arnold Baker, an account director at Publicis (the advertising agency), what he thought constituted brilliance in presenting today. He said that some of the best were utterly shameless, that to them this was show time and that they'd say anything and make up anything to achieve a good effect.

Brilliant presenters should polish their craft and coach those around them. There is too little constructive talk about how to create great presentations, yet this is what often elevates debate about a subject and the advancement of human understanding.

4 The context of the presentation

If you don't know *why* you are doing a presentation, *where* you are doing it, *when* you are doing it, to *whom* you are doing it, *what* the state of the political or commercial climate is, *what* the audience knows already and *what* they expect then expect to fail – unless, of course, you are very, very lucky.

Have you got the plot?

Understanding the context in which your presentation will take place is the single biggest factor in determining whether or not you can become a brilliant presenter. Understand the exact reason for a presentation, the occasion of its happening, the audience desires and needs, the local and world situation, the company's latest news, gossip within the company – never underestimate this – and you may find that a fairly mediocre piece of work can go down a storm.

The impact of context is mighty. What may be a fantastic presentation on day one may sink like a stone on another – the all-important audience reaction is always about context. So how do you avoid getting it wrong and how, on a more positive note, do you make sure you get it right?

First of all get the exam question right

It seems pretty obvious, but do your presentation on the subject you've been asked to talk about. Auberon Waugh was apparently ready, at a price, to talk about virtually anything anytime and anywhere in the world. However, he misheard the organiser of a particular conference over the phone – all he heard really was the word 'Tuscany' followed shortly by the words 'pounds' and 'thousands'. He was then startled to be asked to talk about breast feeding. Nonetheless, Tuscany is Tuscany and thousands of pounds are thousands of pounds so he conscientiously researched the subject about which he'd previously known nothing. It was only in Florence as he was about to deliver that he discovered he was supposed to be talking about press freedom. An easy mistake to make – especially if you are slightly deaf and rather avaricious.

It's astonishing how often this 'exam question problem' is got wrong. Here is a series of pre-planning questions you should ask, and have answered, if you are to maximise your chances of doing yourself justice.

The professional presenter's top ten checklist

1. **What is the event all about?**

   - Why is it happening?

   - Who decided to set it up?

   - What is the agenda?

   - Is there a hidden agenda?

   - What is the organiser hoping to achieve?

   - What is the parent company doing currently?

   - What issues is the company facing – commercially, competitively, strategically, financially, politically, in staff turnover terms, in terms of management stability, new brooms or old brooms, bad news, good news, scandals?

2. **What about the people in the audience?**

   - Do they like each other?

- What happened last time this group got together? Did they stick around afterwards?

- Was the event a success or a failure?

- Are there any underlying tensions? While running one offsite presentation I found the atmosphere very strange. It transpired that the CEO and deputy CEO were at loggerheads, so much so that one would probably have to leave the business. Their colleagues were taking sides. No one had thought to mention all this in briefing me.

- What do the people in the audience do? Are they your subordinates, peers or superiors?

- Does anyone know what they think, what their problems are and what they expect from you and this meeting?

- Do they know you or of you? If so what does this knowledge comprise? If not what is their expectation likely to be?

- Can you get to meet any of them before you speak? David Heslop (ex-CEO Mazda and Expotel) was asked to speak to the sales guys from the *Independent*. He prepared his presentation and then realised that it was full of him, what he thought, his industry not theirs and that if he did get through to them at all then that it would be purely coincidental. He happens to be a good pianist so he arrived a day early and played piano in the hotel bar where, incognito, he got to know many of the *Independent* people. When he spoke next day he did so knowledgeably and as an insider. He was a 'wow'.

3. What size of audience?

- How many will there be in the audience? This is critical – there are broadly four kinds of audience size:

▶

- *intimate meeting* (under 10) – a sit down, relatively informal, board meeting style environment with, hopefully, plenty of interaction. A flip chart or overhead projector can work well, but avoid elaborate and expensive visual aids.

- *big meeting* (10–30) – this is a reasonably formal meeting with fairly strict rules of engagement, which nonetheless will need plenty of back and forth conversation if it is to achieve high energy. This can be a brilliant forum for achieving big realignment of company thinking or strategy.

- *on stage* (30–100) – now we are beginning to talk 'theatre'. You need a stage, good lighting, sound systems and decent visuals. You'll need to have a carefully crafted speech. You may be less likely to improvise and you will need to be more careful.

- *theatre* (100+) – at this level we are talking about all the tricks of the trade. You need professional backup, and if you don't have it in spades then you aren't being professional. Spend at least as much time on rehearsing in situ as you would rehearsing in total for a smaller event. This is high risk and high reward. Someone from Unilever told me about 'the good old days' at the Palladium when top management was expected to perform alongside the likes of Tommy Cooper and Eric Morecambe at big sales presentations. Now that really is quite challenging stuff.

■ A big 'show' is also a big test of you as a manager. If you don't know exactly how that theatre or that stage is going to *feel* then you are running as big a risk as someone going on a journey to a place they've never been before without a map.

4. Where are things heading?

■ Think really hard about the present and the future. We are living in a world of profound change. As Leonard Riggio of Barnes and

Noble put it in *Fast Company*, 'Everything is in play'. This means that no presentation made to any serious management group can have much credibility unless it adequately reflects the scale and pace of current change. You should start every presentation with 'Are you sitting comfortably? Well you shouldn't be.'

- There are many good examples. Google are talking about their developments being constrained by the speed of light! The size of China is put into context when I tell you its disabled population is the same as the total UK population! McDonalds find it quicker, cheaper and more efficient to outsource their customer ordering than to do it on the premises! Hedge funds are now so big that collectively they will, in effect, run the world economy shortly! The older consumers will kill marketing as we know it because they all know how it works — 'pull the other one Paul Daniels!' Most of the technology we rely on today will be redundant by 2010! Big corporations are doomed — they just take a long time to die! Don't know how to use the web? Expire leviathan!

- So are you fully up to speed with the context of the markets within which you operate? You need to be because no one wants to listen to anyone who is out of date.

5. Are you totally up to speed on the day itself?

- By that I mean with what is going on in the news — not just in your business. I was once doing an offsite presentation to a strategy group. As I drove to the meeting I heard the dire news of 'Black Wednesday' unfolding with Norman 'je ne regrette rien' Lamont, addressing the media as interest rates soared. The poor souls at my presentation, having been locked away, knew nothing of this until I told them. From that point on nothing else mattered to them. They all sat quietly and miserably considering their newly unaffordable mortgages. Context is everything.

6. Where is it and what is the agenda?

- In the office, close by, luxury hotel, overnight, abroad, big or small location?

- What sort of room?

- What sort of equipment?

- Do you have any say in what can be changed?

- Do you trust the people running it?

- Will it be hot or cold? Whatever you arrange be comfortable and confident – a tight suit and tie in 35°C is a bad idea. I once gave a presentation to an advertising conference in the Martinez in Cannes. Very hot. Sweltering at 2 p.m. I abandon prepared dress. Focus just on 'look'. Go 'mafia'. Dark glasses. Black suit. Open-necked white linen shirt. Rumpled, bedroom hair. They love the creative look. I talk creatively. . . few words, lots of audience contact. I speak what we now call 'bloke'. We connected.

- Who comes before and after you? How are the audience likely to be feeling as you come on – bored, asleep, dead, excited, argumentative, angry, fed up, happy, expectant, relieved? Whatever it is 'play' to the mood and don't fight it. Context is everything.

7. What is the mood on the day itself?

- The worst mistake any of us make is to judge everything to precision except, as actors would put it, 'the smell of the audience on the night'. Before you start presenting you must judge how people are. If they are edgy and unresponsive – maybe a series of bad car journeys or a star team player had a row before leaving home – sense it and give them all time to settle.

- Perfect performance is not about perfection. What a coup for Neville Coghill and for Oxford – getting Richard Burton right at the peak of his career to come up and play Dr Faustus. It was at the height of his affair with Elizabeth Taylor – double coup as she was billed to play Helen of Troy. Richard Burton was no stranger to drink and he drank a lot beneath the dreaming spires. Rather drunk, he didn't really know his lines – anyone else would have collapsed but … he knew the meaning of the play. It was undoubtedly the definitive Dr Faustus. He performed the core meaning, and if the details got blurred we can forgive gods like this.

8. How do *you* feel?

- Nerves – you've not conquered them but you have controlled them. You are really quite commanding when presenting – people talk of you as a natural performer. Now is the time to pay attention. Imagine that you feel ill – you are sweating, you have an upset stomach, you want to die. . .you are probably dying as you speak, if only the cruel audience knew just how you felt.

- How you feel physically is not the issue. Are you focused and alert and 'up for it' – that's what matters.

9. Do you know what the audience feels?

- Get a feel for what it's like being in the audience by going and sitting where the audience will sit and getting someone else to talk from where you'll be talking.

10. Are you in charge?

- With those management skills you obviously possess you can encourage, cajole and tell the guys who do coffee, tea and lunch to work with you rather than against you.

▶

■ Get there early and have chats with the people who are often ignored. Whatever happens, at least they will be on your side when your presentation starts. A great presentation to a small group was sabotaged (slightly but badly) by the presenter having a silly and undignified disagreement with a waitress who subsequently insisted on pointing at him and loudly describing him as 'that idiot over there.'

If you don't know where you are, you can't really know what you are doing. Nor can you do it – whatever it is – particularly well. I believe that the key skill of a brilliant presenter is to know that they've covered the following questions:

■ Why is it happening?
■ Where is it happening?
■ When is it happening?
■ Who will be listening?
■ What do they want?

5 How to write a great story

Content is king. This is not a book full of elastoplast that teaches you how to busk it (although I can help you do that too). Unless you can learn how to create a good and interesting story it is unlikely you will ever be a very good presenter. The starting point is to get to work on what you want to say, your key message – as I prefer to put it, your 'story'.

A great story

The recent winner of the UK Whitbread prize for literature is by an American, James Shapiro, who claims that he hated Shakespeare at school but is now besotted with him. His book is called *1599* and tells the story of that one year in which William Shakespeare wrote, among other things, *Henry V*, *Julius Caesar*, *As You Like It* and *Hamlet* – not bad for one year's output, not bad stories.

Now when I talk about the need to 'tell a story' I am not counselling you to emulate Shakespeare (although you could do much worse than try) but I am asking you to give me a sense of narrative drive where there is a strong beginning, a coherent middle and a powerful, surprising and memorable ending. In other words, have a tale worth telling.

Death to mission statements and other jargon

As I said earlier, in one of the organisations that I chair I have banned the use of that ghastly phrase 'mission statement' and have insisted it is replaced by 'our story' as I am convinced that this will encourage people away from corporate speak, jargon and bullet points towards simplicity, excitement and commonsense.

The great thing about stories is, after all, that they have something to say.

Ten top tips for creating your story

1. Start by deciding what the 'end' is – what the final point is that you want to make.

2. Everything you do must lead up to this final point – everything.

3. Limit your thinking to the 'rule of three' – in this simple technique you are *never* allowed to use more than three points. Try it and see how powerful it is. For example, there are just three things to say about creating a story – stories are designed to command the attention of the audience; stories are about people, things and events; and all stories are about change.

4. Ironically, at this point I, of course, immediately break the rule of three by moving through my fourth and on to my fifth point. As you get better at presenting remember that rules can be broken.

5. Try to summarise the key thrust of your story in just a few words – a kind of elevator pitch. For example, in saying 'this presentation is about our growth, how we've achieved it and what we are going to do next' this will 'fix' in your mind the journey you are going to take. Many of us find it hard to say exactly where we are going, which probably accounts for the fact that so few of us actually get there.

6. Make your story sound fresh and new – as if it has only just happened, and also as though it has happened to you.

7. Give your audience the setting for the story in graphic terms – time, place, temperature, ambience and so on – hook into people's

imagination. Do you remember those stories that started 'It was a dark and stormy night'?

8. Be ruthless about cutting out anything in your presentation, however nice you think it is, which doesn't drive the story on.

9. Try to create a simple structure so that the presentational story has an order to it. Something like: 1 This is where we were; 2 This is where we are now; 3 This is where we want to be.

10. Depending on the context of your story, try to introduce first person experiences and anecdotes. For example, I remember a powerful story I told the DHSS when I was in advertising and we pitched for a teenage anti-smoking campaign. It was about my niece who was given cigarettes by her mother when she went to parties so that if she felt that she really had to smoke she wasn't put at risk of being given one laced with skunk by a friend. This anecdote spoke volumes to ministers and their officials.

A way of thinking about your story is to regard it as the framework around which everything else fits. It's a simple truth that if you haven't got a good story to tell then you haven't got a good presentation.

> IF YOU HAVEN'T GOT A GOOD STORY TO TELL THEN YOU HAVEN'T GOT A GOOD PRESENTATION

The truth is a powerful weapon

We are all impressed by what we rather admiringly call 'true stories'. These are narratives that sound as though they might be fictional –

'you're never going to believe this . . .' – but are grounded in reality and actually happened.

Anecdote wins hands down in a contest with data when it comes to presentations. The politician who personalises his story with an account of a real event grabs the headlines. Presentations in business will be based, almost by definition, on truth and, hopefully, they will be (unless of course you are Enron). How do you turn a liturgy of figures and mission statements (oh dear!) into a narrative, a story that commands attention, inspires belief and, hopefully, takes the business forward?

The advice I've given already should help but if you want to achieve brilliance then you have to go a bit further than simply applying a mechanical process. You'll have to learn how that interaction between story, storyteller and audience works.

Does the story grab the imagination?

Martin Conradi, CEO of Showcase, proposed the 'mother test.' First find a mother – any mother will do – and tell her your story. If she understands it and is interested by it you are probably on to a winner – if, however, she does neither then start again. Martin might well have suggested the 'small child test' because it is young children who are the most fearless of critics and the most expert in the art of sussing out a good or bad story.

In the golden youthful era of storytelling, the acid test of a good story is whether or not it inspires – the Harry Potter phenomenon is proof enough of that. In our sophisticated, high-tech world a series of tales of low-level witchcraft have dazzled a generation or two, or more. It has also shown how many adults have 'childlike' minds – they are none the worse for that either. When *Harry Potter and the Half-Blood Prince* came out it went to the top of the best-seller lists in France and Germany – not the French or German versions (published about eight months later) but in English. Picture the poor young folks in Marseille or Munich reading this 600-page tome slow word by slow word just to get their heads round the story.

Become a story student

Listen to the stories that people tell at work, at home, in the pub – wherever. Work out why some work and some fail. Listen to comedians and watch the news. Become a 'story addict'. Learn what seems to work and then adopt the role of storyteller and finally try to grip the attention of your audience through the simplicity, conviction and narrative drive of your performance.

> GRIP THE ATTENTION OF YOUR AUDIENCE THROUGH THE SIMPLICITY, CONVICTION AND NARRATIVE DRIVE OF YOUR PERFORMANCE

Practise, practise, practise – it takes time but keep at it. And don't forget to try it on your mother or on a child. Set yourself a 'story test'. Keep on asking yourself if the story you are telling is:

- interesting
- relevant
- accurate
- involving
- clear
- well structured
- memorable
- making demands on your audience – you do want them to do something as a result of it don't you?

The best presentations were great stories

Some of the best presentations I've heard have been stories of discovery and learning. Others have been sermons – one of the great art forms of all time where a ten-minute story should be designed to make you laugh and frown, and think and remember at a series of different levels.

But the best I ever heard came from Tony O'Reilly. He was talking to the Marketing Society at the Royal Lancaster Hotel in London about German retailing in 1990. He played the Irish British Lion card brilliantly – rugby, Brendan Behan and drinking stories. As a raconteur this man has it all. He looks good, he's rich, he's famous, he's been a great sportsman and he's very funny. Since then he's got richer – a lot richer – and probably funnier too.

I loved the, probably, apocryphal story of him at Heinz as a very young man determined to win brownie points for his keenness from a workaholic boss. He'd get in really early – say 6.30 a.m. – and be there head down when his boss passed by shortly after 7.00 a.m. Having established his presence he crept off to a quiet part of the building for an hour's snooze at about 7.15 a.m. That's style. It's also quite sensible.

Great memory hook but what's the story?

One of the most interesting presentations I ever went to was at M&C Saatchi's Golden Square offices one Sunday where the School of Economic Science put on an event . They had really good speakers at the first session I went to – Sir David Putnam, Professor Paul Robertson (spectacularly brilliant on the effects of Mozart on autistic children) and the actress Emily Watson.

On this occasion Graham Fink spoke – now Creative Director of M&C Saatchi but then founder of a creative business called the Fink Tank. Graham spoke well and without notes but rather nervously – a precursor to David Cameron, currently leader of the Conservative Party. I remember that he showed us some ads, that he also urgently stressed the importance of creativity, asserting that he is very creative (which he is), and that he had a middle-aged lady with her hair done up in a scarf sat on stage knitting and ignoring what was going on around her. She subsequently turned out to be Fink's mother. The reason she was there was to capture our attention. She was charming but her presence was as relevant as that line in recent esure commercials, 'Don't worry dear, it's only a commercial.'

What a story!

Michael Mayne, ex-Dean of Westminster followed Graham Fink. He was heavily scripted, and he read it – each word – but every word was pregnant with meaning. He was completely brilliant in describing the story of how transcendental experiences could be obtained, in virtually equal measure, from great art, great music, great poetry and from spiritual experiences themselves. He read from Milton, played Mozart, described or showed paintings. The whole experience was magical – a cornucopia of pleasures heard, as it were, sitting at the feet of a mightier, albeit humble, human being. I thought Michael was a complete genius.

Yet when we spoke afterwards he said that he was bemused to be juxtaposed with Mr. Fink, saying that he hadn't understood what he'd been talking about or why everyone had seemed to take him so seriously. I explained that I could speak with authority on the subject – that ads had their place, that ads were indeed fine but flippant by nature because they were transient and that Shakespeare, Mozart, Rembrandt and God might prove to be just a touch more timeless!

Another great storyteller is Tom Peters whose power of delivery may be a greater factor in his success than his ability to forensically dissect a management situation. Yet he tells power story after power story quite compellingly. I also love his own story – imagine, he said, your own gravestone. What he wants on his is 'Tom Peters – he was a player'. Perfect.

I heard him in Amsterdam recently and I thought he was great. He made quite brilliant use of anecdote and of his vivid experiences in real companies like South Western Airlines. It was incidentally Herb Kelleher, the one time CEO of South Western, who uttered the down-to-earth immortal line, devoid of jargon, 'Yeah we have a strategy at

South Western – we do things.' So the next time you're preparing for a presentation steal this directness – 'Yeah I'm going to do a presentation – I have a story to tell.'

Remember, next time you present, that if you haven't got a story then you haven't got a presentation – 'Yes . . . do I have a story to tell!'

6 How to give your story colour

There are more and more good presenters out there today. Their 'presenting' is earning them promotion and new jobs. They are developing their careers on stage. While they may have mastered many aspects of presenting, real competitive edge can only be gained by the unusual ability to give your story and your presentation a splash of colour.

A nearly great presentation in the making

Suppose you have a good story that withstands the pressure of interrogation and that obeys all the key tenets of presenting:

- it is relevant to your audience;
- it has a very clear message;
- you applied the 'less is more' rule ruthlessly to the point that it is now incredibly cryptic;
- it is ten minutes long even though they asked for half an hour;
- it has no detours, no irrelevance, no shades of anything but grey.

In short it has a great framework and is likely to be as dull as tap water – totally clear with just a faint back taste of urine (well, this presentation sounds as though it has been through about 30 audiences already).

Anyone could do this – even a Dalek. Actually a Dalek might do it even better.

A bare presentation is like bare walls

This chapter is about helping to put the intellectual ornaments and rhetorical colouring into your simple story – the stuff that will turn it from being a plot line into a narrative that engages the audience's mind. Something with shades of colour and emphasis. Something with highlights and lowlights with solid logic and emotional intelligence which has a certainty of destination, but with surprises en route.

> THE STUFF THAT WILL TURN IT FROM BEING A PLOT LINE INTO A NARRATIVE THAT ENGAGES THE AUDIENCE'S MIND

So how do you find these embellishments? As Dylan Thomas said, 'let's start at the beginning.'

Ten top tips for decorating your presentation

1. **Work at breakfast time** – read as many papers as you can. Focus on the *Financial Times*, *The Times* and the *Sun*. But always read *The Week* and *Private Eye* too. Snip out any good stories. One of the things that freshens any story is something contemporary, something that's just happened, something recent that demonstrates a point you want to make. Be totally ruthless in choosing a story that makes you look up to date – best of all, of course, is the statement of the type 'this appeared in today's FT –what do you make of it? Let me make just three points about it . . .'

   There's something about 'morning fresh' that is totally captivating. It positions you as an on-the-ball person.

2. **Read the big management books** – you have no choice as an aspiring 'big-time-brilliant presenter' but to be an avid consumer of

the key, current management books – from Tom Peters to Jack Welch, Jim Collins to Patrick Lencioni, Michael Heppell through to a much longer list. These are people who will give you insights, thoughts or who will simply give you amazing slides. You don't have to read all these cover to cover of course – just learn to be a great scanner.

Look for the big thought or quote – and keep one eye open for a big idea.

3. **Look out for big pictures** – these are around us all the time but we'd seldom either think or have the courage to use them – pictures of 7/7 or of the World Cup or the Ryder Cup. Some will be corny and some contemporary. Some will be pictures you've seen before – the *Laughing Cavalier*, the *Scream*, the *Mona Lisa*, Picasso's *Guernica*, Hurst's *Sheep*, Tracy Emin's *Bed*. Look out for the great news pictures, especially recent ones which will resonate with your audience. Also look out for visual treats in the papers – study the *Financial Times* who, at their best, do some awesome design work with financial results.

There is nothing more colourful and exciting than to be taken on a big adventurous presentational journey.

4. **Do you have a real sense of curiosity?** – it may have killed the cat but as sure as anything I know in business it makes a business presentation sing. Curiosity delivers quirky insights, it is the lead-in to discovering the unusual, the story or fact which can captivate an audience. Curiosity's currency is the line made famous by Michael Caine, 'and not many people know that.' Someone asked me what I mean by 'being curious'. What I mean is keeping your eyes open and seeing what's changed, what's stayed the same, what's died, what's been born, what's been relaunched.

▶

Become a question machine and an accumulator of oddball stories. Read *Google Zeitgeist*. Look. Listen. Question.

5. **Keep an 'ideas' book beside you** – you have to keep a book in which the great quotes and insights you gather are kept. Not because you are a train spotter but because you never know when they might be useful in fleshing out a presentation. For example, you are talking about the importance of speed in business today – Mario Andretti, the great Formula One driver, said 'If you're in control you aren't going fast enough.' Now that's similar to the comment made to the British ice skating champion Robin Cousins who was told that he wasn't going to make it because 'he didn't skate to fall'. Consider both of these quotes and what they mean. Could you do a presentation just focusing on these two quotes? Or suppose there's been a corporate marriage. I love this, by Anthony Hilton in the *Evening Standard* on takeovers and mergers, 'the lunch comes immediately; the bill comes later'.

6. **Do you have a killer chart?** – Jack Welch tells stories of how he and his colleagues spent hours trying to refine just one chart which encapsulated a whole strategic thought. Finding a way of talking about, say, a new people-strategy may be as arid as the Sahara in bullet points but in contrasting the two shapes or – if your people are really clever – morphing from a triangle (normal structure) to say a circle (twenty-first century structure) may say more things more quickly and more clearly than you can imagine.

   Besides which, interesting material and visual material can be more interesting for you to talk to. Too many words on screen can slow you down.

7. **Agendas are a key to expectation** – ironically most people regard the agenda as a necessary extra that sits rather drably in the 'conference housekeeping drawer'. But how would you feel about a

restaurant with a scruffy menu? Your agenda *is* your menu. Treat it as the way of previewing how the meeting is going to be – serious and data filled, fun and innovative, about people, about the future or a review of the past. It's the dustcover to the book you are going to launch so treat it with great respect and produce something that looks colourful, well-thought out, attention-getting and important. At recent meetings we've had laminated agendas, pocket-sized agendas, bookmark agendas – anything that takes you from the prosaic.

The next one will be circular, or we might print it on an inflatable. Well that would be a great way of doing an agenda for a global conference.

8. **Takeaways are reminders of the event** – at analysts' meetings you need presentation printouts on which they can make their copious notes. But these represent a small part of all the meetings and presentations that most people have to do. What every presentation needs is an elegant follow-up, and I love what Martin Conradi at Showcase invented – he calls them 'lunch-books'. They are called this because they are ring bound, A5 and easy to handle so you can use them while having lunch without knocking the water over or anything else. They contain the slides and as many appendices as are necessary.

A good takeaway puts the gloss on a great presentation. Perhaps more importantly it can revive a poor one. Also remember to get everyone to leave their card so you can easily follow things up and you can turn an audience into a lifelong network.

9. **The power of the 'money shot'** – there is that moment in every Bond movie that has people sitting on the edge of their seats– one that everyone tells their friends about, 'So-so movie but that bit where they go over the glacier on a snowmobile is incredible'. In the

▶

same way with presentations we are looking for charismatically memorable effects. Now these are not *always* appropriate, especially with small audiences where pyrotechnics will seem superfluous. But with larger audiences you need not only that killer slide but also that high impact moment – maybe borrowed from a favourite film. Maybe it's animation. We did a fairly corny but very effective 'tipping point' animation recently using a seesaw that is incredibly hard to move until – whoops – suddenly it tips and all else follows. Corny but memorable.

Look to have a moment in your presentation you are looking forward to presenting – a moment to remember.

10. **Always involve the audience** – I was asked recently how this could be achieved at a relatively small seminar, and when I said 'give them sweets' I think she thought I'd gone mad. Of course, what I was suggesting was interaction. Sweets, chocolates – anything like that would do – sampling drinks if it's relevant. Sampling an ordinary Bordeaux and a great New World wine both selling at the same price is a great way of starting a presentation or a debate on the new order and how things are changing today. To make it really interesting you could include Great Wall wine from China too – old world, new world, next world. Now that's a scary presentation to which I really want to come. Give them ice cream if it's hot and lead a debate on climate change – then do your presentation but with interruptions and questions encouraged as you go along. Take risks, be imaginative, run polls on issues – electronically – it creates amazing tensions and excitements and, for some reason, we all love scores. Do live interviews – get people up on stage – get roaming mikes around the audience.

Become a compere not just a presenter.

These are the 'big tips' but I also want you and your team to think your way towards being more colourful.

- **Be fresh** – a presentation will nearly always be enhanced by individualised splashes of colour because it will appear to be 'freshly cooked', as opposed to being ready prepared in some presentation factory or, worse still, a leftover from a previous meeting.

- **Think creatively about your presentation** – we live in a world of increasing sophistication. Most of us are processing more and more arcane pieces of information. They used to say that information is power. This may be true for Google, but for the rest of us clarity of thought and creativity are what are really powerful and information is merely there to be used. So use it – use it to intrigue and to educate; use it to make your presentations more fun and more lively.

> CLARITY OF THOUGHT AND CREATIVITY ARE WHAT ARE REALLY POWERFUL AND INFORMATION IS MERELY THERE TO BE USED

- **Thinking on your feet is colourful in itself** – one of the most exciting presentations I ever saw that was crammed with colour was by Marybeth Moss Kantor who ran a masterclass in strategy at the London Business School. Her flashes of colour were all intellectual but not everyone is as clever as she is.

- **Nearly too late** – and the most difficult I have done myself was to a roomful of Chinese, Russians and Iranians in Shenzen at the Global Holography Conference. I had two simultaneous translators sitting in what looked like a Tardis at the end of the room, along with 300 slides operated by a green-faced (because she felt so sick with nerves) Chinese girl – an MA from Warwick University as I discovered – who confessed, just before we embarked on the three-hour talk, that she had never done this but she did brilliantly – one small flaw in 300 slides – hey that's a top six sigma score. There was no technical run through – the Chinese are not used to such things. My language was quite colourful too as I recall. This was a classic example of 'just in time' becoming 'nearly too late'.

The moral is to ask these key questions of yourself and your team at that first critical meeting, when you are writing the brief – 'How do we make this presentation totally different, one that is quite different from expectation and that has a real wow factor?' 'How do we, as a team, find those splashes of colour that will have the audience saying "good plot overall – but I also love the writing"?'

7 How to illustrate your presentation

Opera – great story, great music, great performance by the cast. There is a powerful simplicity to many operatic stories. Great visual aids, like the music in opera, can take your rhetoric and argument to a higher level than if you simply rely on the spoken word.

Think of slides as your music

Even if you don't actually have any slides, don't for one moment imagine that you are doing an unillustrated presentation – if you have no visual aids you have made a decision to make *yourself* the illustration. How you look, what you wear and the way you behave will have even more importance than normal.

Bad slides slow you down

Curiously, many people seem to regard slides as a mere adjunct to a presentation – a kind of necessary evil. Good and sharp visuals help to drive a presentation, making it easier to understand and more compelling than if there were none, but poor visuals slow everything down – like trying to drive with the handbrake on.

> POOR VISUALS SLOW EVERYTHING DOWN – LIKE TRYING TO DRIVE WITH THE HANDBRAKE ON

Equally, while anyone can cobble themselves together a half decent, conventional kind of presentation, many are fettered by bullet points – the presentational equivalent of sleeping policemen.

Professional slides make a presentation sing

On the other hand, a really skilled operator can, with experience, make a PowerPoint presentation look wonderful. I used to work in advertising and there was one piece of advice I consistently gave clients, 'Don't try to do your own advertising'. As with DIY surgery, the result will not necessarily be what you would wish.

By the same token make sure that you get well-trained and experienced people to finish off your visuals if you want them to have great impact. Don't try to do them yourself – unless, of course, the casual, amateur look is something you want to project.

Professorial vagueness has its place

Interestingly, many academics seem to be happiest with scratched, out of order and apparently frequently changed overheads. These create a very public denunciation of style. So far as they are concerned they are saying that substance and work in progress is all that matters. Do we imagine that Newton would have had a very snazzy presentation with gorgeous shots of apples? Or would it have been a rather old envelope? Or more like the erratic genius Robin Hankey, who I knew at Oxford, who wrote his essays from west to east and then turned the paper round 90 degrees and carried on writing north to south over the previous text?

We return to scrutiny of the context of a presentation if we want to decide on the most appropriate visual techniques and the amount of money we want to spend.

Less is more

In general terms I advocate a 'less is more' approach. Keep the number of slides down to perhaps one a minute, or even 45 seconds. Go for maximum focused impact and minimal words. Consider animation. Include video if you can – talking, for instance, about a retail outlet while watching a possibly speeded up video of it can work much more powerfully than looking at a sales graph. Consider big, bold, single word slides like this:

$$\text{FOCUS}$$

You have to concede it gets your attention!

A favourite of mine involved a presentation for a firm of accountants and we wanted to talk about the benefits of partnership – how working together, client and accountant, could achieve synergistic benefits. This was the slide that did that:

$$2 + 2 = 5$$

So how do you set about this?

Ten top tips to get you started on your slides

1. **Always start with your story** – always know what you are saying, to whom and what you want to achieve. Showing pictures of stormtroopers with the slogan 'Let's go get 'em' may not be that helpful in a presentation about partnership and stakeholder relationships. The pictures have to illustrate the story you are telling, not something else.

2. **Decide how big an impact you want** – how many in the audience, how big a hall, how smart and attuned an audience, language difficulties (more of this later). Your slides need more impact the bigger the hall.

▶

3. **Your voice; your style** – I have a personal antipathy to corporate templates which nearly always swamp the presenter's good intentions in what I describe as 'corporate porridge'. Yet I am a lifelong advocate of brand values. I am a passionate fan of Heinz with whom I've worked on many projects over the years. You don't need to slam 'H.J. Heinz' at the bottom of every slide with bullets shaped like the famous keystone to make it look like a Heinz presentation. Indeed, the best presentation I ever saw from them was done smartly without such constraints and yet it breathed that sense of 'there's no taste like Heinz' in a way that a more mechanistic offering could never have done. If you are not doing a corporate but more a personal presentation, decide in a focused – almost a feminine – way on your 'look'. This involves font, colours, feel and style. There is a later chapter in the book which warns against using exotic and mysterious fonts in case in the transportation of a presentation from one computer to another the font is not recognised. I discovered such a font recently which, for obvious reasons, looked good to me on my computer – it is called 'Poor Richard' and here's how it appeared on another PC – ✎ ℳ ■ 𝑒𝑟 ☜ ○ ℋ ■! Avoid indulgences such as 'Poor Richard' like the plague – life is hard enough without being a presentational punk.

4. **You need toys to play with** – not everything visual has to appear on a screen. Assuming that it was relevant, you might put a packet of jelly beans on the seat of every member of the audience, or a specially created agenda – or if you're talking about innovation and you want to explore that wow factor why not put a 'WOW' card on every seat for the audience to wave whenever they feel a wow moment (just as cricket spectators seem to wave big 4s when a boundary is scored). Nick Horswell, ex-colleague and founder of the media company PHD, once did a presentation which climaxed (I'm not entirely sure that is the right word) in his walking off stage

trouserless from behind the lectern having walked on stage fully trousered. I'm not sure how he did it, undoing his pants and still giving a decent presentation, but he did. Suffice to say that trousers-down Horswell also brought the house down.

5. **Making the experience seem real** – if you are talking about a product, work out how to make the product 'hero'. Years ago I met Jilly Cooper when I was working on a new account – Jeyes, one of whose products was Sanilav. I was very young, impressionable and very enthusiastic. Hell, I even ate half an Airwick solid air freshener in front of an astonished account team to prove how pure and safe it was. I solemnly emptied the loo cleaner into a Dartington glass tumbler where it fizzed blue and angrily. Jilly mused that I looked like a thirsty man about to drink a gin and tonic. I remember feeling so strongly that there had never been a better, bluer loo cleaner. The lesson is, wherever you can, to use products. Pass them round. Make people see them close up, touch them and taste them. Don't just let them sit there lifeless on a screen.

6. **Enjoy doing your slides** – think of things from the audience's point of view. Think about how to get them on your side, about colour, about simple points. Can you get pictures of any of your audience on screen? Or of the buyer of your product at Tesco? Something that speaks to your audience. If you sit down and think of this as hard work and boring it will show.

7. **A picture is worth 10,000 words** – but obviously it has to be the right picture. If a presenter is talking about, say, productivity and a picture of a carrot appears on the screen then the audience is likely to be a bit baffled. I recently did a presentation in China which, given the language issues, had to be predominantly visual. The key point is, of course, that finding great visuals that begin to tell a story is very, very time consuming. I and three researchers spent an indecently long time scouring the internet to find exactly what I wanted.

▶

8. **The tour de force** – this is the sort of thing the ever-brilliant Richard Eyres, now a non-executive director at the Guardian Media Group, has used in presentations. I've seen him do a great presentation in which he talked, among other things, about the creation of the Capital Radio website (it had to be 'not leading edge or even cutting edge – it had to be bleeding edge' according to the designers). An executive from Pearson, as I recall hearing it told to me, did a very energetic presentation with a new slide every seven seconds or so. 'Don't do it' begged the producers. But he did. And I'm told it was a complete wow. Sometimes you have to go for it.

9. **Don't make it all the same** – what can look like a neat, clear presentation as a booklet to be taken away can be the equivalent of a monotonic drone presented on the big screen. Presentation is theatre … with pauses … with lows and highs, fast bits and slooowwweeerr bits. The visual impact of your presentation can catapult you to the heights or, if it's boring, act like the deadweight of a sea anchor.

10. **Compiling a brief in cryptic words and pictures** – your designer can't really be expected to read your script and immediately understand what you are trying to achieve. So get a few A5 sheets and create a series of simplistic charts with a thick felt tip pen. This is a Showcase trick which stops you putting too many words on a slide. No more than 8–10 words to a slide is ideal – the best creative directors in advertising used to claim no poster should have more than 5–6 words, so check out some of today's posters. See how you get on being this reductive. Then try it again seeing if you can spot opportunities for some visual fun. Then again to see if the slides tell your story. If you need special emphasis then indicate where this is. Now you are ready to brief your presentation designer.

Why people avoid slides

There are many reasons why so many presenters are nervous of slides.

- Except when they were under five, they have always been used to verbal and written communication, not visual.

- They wouldn't know a good piece of visual communication if it bit them on the leg.

- The moment something goes on a slide, technology gets involved and anything can happen. A guy at Royal Bank of Scotland Insurance had rehearsed his big set piece presentation – it was at a foreign location. He'd have scored A+ for preparation. He went up on stage and the people running the show managed to let their computer go down. Blank screen – crisis! Fortunately he had the sang-froid to chill it out. They rebooted and off he went again – 'whew!'

- It isn't just technology, it's about control – 'I'd rather have average PowerPoint slides I've done myself that I can change at the last minute'. I know what you mean but you don't really, really mean it? Not really. Mediocre is not what an aspiring brilliant presenter wants to be.

It's all a bit like President Gerald Ford, who it was said couldn't walk and chew gum at the same time. You have a lot to do and a lot to remember – you have your nerves to conquer, your words to say, things to remember and slides to pay attention to – something's going to crash.

Possibly the worst presentation – but there are so many, OK one of the worst – was when I saw a nervous ad man go off at pace pressing his own slide button. This was before the age of computers and he managed to go the wrong way, so the final slide came up first and his 'Welcome' slide came up last. The slides and his words bore no relation to each other. Having been told never to look behind you at the screen he didn't, and so had no idea what was going on. There were quiet mutterings among the audience, and then laughter which he thought was at a joke and this just encouraged him the more. He speeded up –

he shouted 'Sales will grow' to the accompaniment of a half-dressed girl lying on the bonnet of a car with the headline 'Big Engines are a Turn On'. People in the audience stood up and shouted. He just got louder and faster. Someone approached the stage and tried to help but the presenter resisted exclaiming 'I will have my say'.

Whether or not you use slides consider the following.

- You are in trouble if you don't find out if those before and after you are using them or not. An audience who have just experienced half an hour of blazing visual pyrotechnics will feel odd trying to adjust to seeing you standing there with a blank screen. Don't you care? Didn't you have time to produce any slides? Do you prefer mono as opposed to 3-d presentations? You'll have to be really good to over-come the negative no-slide-impact you'll create.

- If you don't use slides then *you* are the visual. Everyone will look at you intently, so you'd better be very interesting or very important. Or else exciting – no need for handstands, but do deliver an inter-esting mix of pitch, pace and movement.

- You can hide behind the lectern but then they will focus just on your face. This scenario could be very dull unless your content and delivery are riveting and you have a great voice. It will help to keep things very brief – it is ill-advised for any stand-up speech without slides, however good, to last for more than 8–10 minutes.

- If you do use slides then understand that a dramatic change in the presentational dynamic is achieved. You have stopped being the star – you are the voice-over. No one is looking at you – they are staring at the screen. And if you care about your appearance then care about your slides – when the audience looks at them they are assessing you.

> IF YOU CARE ABOUT YOUR APPEARANCE
> THEN CARE ABOUT YOUR SLIDES

- Poor slides are the presentational equivalent of scuffed shoes, a dirty crumpled shirt and a curry-stained tie.

Are you ever allowed to be boring?

In a word, no. But you are allowed to set up and control a PowerPoint presentation yourself and deliver it sparingly to small audiences provided that you:

- have very few slides;
- use very big words;
- include quotes (these are always good);
- speak interestingly and excitedly to them.

Quite simply, life is too short for boring presentations, boring ads, boring people. We live in a post-boring world, one in which stand-up presentations are the norm. The standards are rising. What was considered to be a brilliant presentation twenty years ago is probably merely good by today's standards.

The one element that has really come on is visual design. All kinds of tricks are possible now in this wonderful age of special effects. Realise that your slides complement your voice and if you really seek brilliance pay really careful attention to them and their production. Let the 'visual voice' have space and time for expression. Done well it will add a dramatic dimension to the other brilliant aspects of your presentations.

8 Performance

How you put yourself across to your audience is going to be key. No, you are not expected to be a completely professional performer but you are expected to perform. You are expected to put on a bit of a show because that's what presentations need – a bit of underlining, a bit of *drama*, a bit of *swagger*. Remember that the audience wants you to wow them. Don't let them down.

What acting can do

Dustin Hoffman takes his job very seriously indeed. When he was in *Marathon Man* he had to appear in one scene completely exhausted. Ever the perfectionist, he stayed up all night and arrived on the set the next day white, puffy eyed and completely knackered. Laurence Olivier surveyed him in amusement, 'Why don't you try acting dear boy? It's so much easier.'

In praise of work – in praise of America

While Britain was a nation admiring Raffles, the Americans were creating Rockefellers. While Britain was defending an empire they were building an economy. They worked incredibly hard – they still do. They don't dream the 'American dream' – they create it brick by brick. Their success is founded on a quite astonishing attention to detail. Whenever you hear people knock the USA remember their work ethic.

So it was with Al Pacino when he performed Shakespeare's *Richard III*. Pacino gathered the cast around and dissected the text word by word examining meaning and motive until it became clearer and clearer what was going on. Shakespeare, he told his exhausted fellow thespians, wasn't casual or sloppy. If a word was there it was there for a reason.

So it is with presenting – if a word is there it must be there for a reason. Getting it right will only be achieved by rigorous questioning and a refusal to stop until you get to the bottom of an issue. I recommend such rigour to you in preparing a presentation. If you work in an American company you will find that exhaustive examination of every word and nuance is commonplace.

Illogical arguments show up in a presentation

Don't be sloppy in building your argument and in creating the logic of your story. At least one acid test of building a credible presentation lies in the practice of constantly interrogating the logic and the flow. The key question is 'Does the argument hold water?' *not* 'Is this good rhetoric?'

Don't go to bed until you've cracked it. Remember *Marathon Man*. Toyota created 'the five whys' as their process of inquisition whereby any proposal was intellectually tortured until it confessed to its weakness, or alternately survived through the strength of its own truth, convictions and logic. For example, suppose that a young executive has a proposal for his company to launch a new range of premium organic chilled meals. His boss is sceptical.

■ **Why** are you making this proposal when our resources are already overstretched?

   Because research shows there's a big gap in the market for this concept, and it is very high margin so there's an incremental volume and profit opportunity. And I'll put in extra time myself to make sure it gets done. The resource issue is down to me and my time.

- **Why** is no one else in this sector – doesn't this suggest there may be something they know that we don't?

  Because it's hard to get the product right, because there's a difficult trade sell to do (but I know we can do this) and because no one else has the organic credentials that we do so our competitors are wisely steering clear. Anyway I think we're a bit smarter than them.

- **Why** do you think that we can overcome trade antipathy, which you concede is a problem, and also live with a potential private label offering? If Tesco were to agree with your market diagnosis they could simply go and do it themselves – and probably would.

  Because if we can get Tesco to stock, in addition to the easier targets like Sainsbury and Waitrose – and I think we can because the taste tests on our product are so exceptional – then the organic story plus our pricing makes this a compelling must-stock range. They might do a Tesco Finest but that would be no big deal.

- **Why** should we do this and run the risk of cannibalising our historically successful, but currently static and under margin-pressure, non-organic offering?

  Because it's all down to positioning isn't it? If we launch head to head against ourselves then you have a strong point, but if we aim more upmarket and go for those already organically predisposed and avoid any recipe duplication then we should be OK.

- **Why** would you want to put your career on the line now, just when you are in line for promotion? You see if this fails to hit plan your life here is over, and I doubt if any of our competitors would be too impressed either. Will you think about that?

  That's a very strong point boss and very well made. Can I go away and have a think about it? What sort of promotion did you actually have in mind by the way?

Why? Why?? Why??? Why???? Why?????

This technique will usually find the weak point in an argument, a position or a presentation. Try it on the argument you assemble for your next presentation. Through laziness or because we can't quite make the argument compute, most of us make jumps in our logic, bury issues which don't suit our argument or, if we are politicians, sometimes fib. Sometimes we even tell really big porkies just to get a brilliant presentation away – sometimes 2 + 2 = 5 because we can't be bothered to do the simple arithmetic.

> SOMETIMES WE EVEN TELL REALLY BIG PORKIES JUST TO GET A BRILLIANT PRESENTATION AWAY

A strong argument helps you feel confident in performance

Your performance deserves a strong and bulletproof argument (as opposed to just bullet point). Not only will it always be better if it has this, it will also be easier to perform – no more butterflies about being destroyed during questions and answers because of an intellectually corrupt flow of logic.

So let's consider the main ways in which performance can be advanced so that you stand out as a presenter. At this stage there will be those among you who say that you hate acting. If this is the case there is little I can do for you. But remember, corporate life nowadays involves a degree of acting.

Ten top tips to make you perform brilliantly

1. **Be yourself, just a bigger you** – David Abbott, one of the legendary advertising figures of the twentieth century, spoke with contempt of

people going into presentation-speak, hunched up, glazed eyes, Dalek-voiced and didactic. Well there's no need for that. Just do a bit of self-examination – of the way you look, the way you move, the way you sound and your very presence. This is quite a hard thing to pin down but there are people who have authority and those who don't – those who inspire trust and those who don't. Take what you have and make a vow to lift yourself up two or three levels.

Be bigger. Impose. But don't be someone else. Especially don't be Mr. Hectoring.

2. **Work on your voice** – it's your single biggest asset – or liability. For most audiences it's all that exists of you when you give a 'whiz bang' slide presentation. How do you feel about your voice? Personally I like and I lean on mine. It sounds deep and strong and it gives me confidence – I can play with its range and pace. When it isn't quite there, through a cold or a surprise attack of nerves, my whole sense of self-belief begins to flutter. Your voice is as important to you as a presenter as your putting stroke is to you as a golfer – so look after it. Record yourself and listen to yourself. Work with a coach if necessary – and it probably is. Someone who slows you down, who makes you speak in lower bass tones. Look at what Gordon Reece managed to do for Margaret Thatcher – she was transformed from a Finchley housewife politician who, as Minister of Education, stopped school milk ('Margaret Thatcher – school milk snatcher') to a world statesperson who spoke with gravitas and passion. The late Edward Heath had voice coaching with the same result – extremely statesmanlike burr.

3. **Work on how you look** – of course you need help, how can you work this out yourself? Get advice on how to dress – for women a well-cut trouser suit always looks powerful and modern; for men a dark suit with a white or light blue shirt and no tie (though of course

you can if you want). Slight sun tan – no workaholic you – always better without glasses but if you do wear them have enough pairs to give a range of impressions from severe to magisterial, from mischievous to intellectual. Do not let anyone, however well intentioned, make you wear anything or have a look that you find makes you feel awkward. The whole point about this is to make you feel better about yourself – you are the star.

You need to think and feel that you look your best to be your best.

4. **Do you have stage presence?** Look around you as you go on stage – the bigger the stage, the bigger the look and the bigger the sweep of your gaze. Walk on with a straight back. However you really feel, look as though you are glad to be there – it's worth repeating that, look as though you are glad to be there. Smile and say 'Ha!' under your breath – especially under your breath if you are miked-up – it will animate your face. If it's a smaller event simply try to be engaged and interested in what is going on and when you start or stand up to speak make a few eye contacts and think 'Hey, I really like these people'. It's amazing how this communicates to an audience. The number of times I've seen ill-at-ease, shifty, grumpy or even downright hostile speakers is legion. Try to imagine that the people out there have loads of money and that they are going to give some to you, but only if you look cheerful and glad to be with them. Stage presence is like sex appeal – some people have it naturally, some acquire it. Whenever Marilyn Monroe stepped into a room everyone stopped and noticed – and that wasn't just because she had big boobs.

5. **Do you radiate self-belief?** As someone once said to me, 'You have to believe what you are saying even if you don't believe it.' What is it that marks out the brilliant presenter? The best presenters in the advertising business tend to be shameless showmen. 'Shameless' is

such a great word – say it to yourself next time you walk up on stage, 'Hey I feel totally shameless today', and see what happens. All you do have to do is radiate confidence and a conviction about your subject. Lord Denning, one of the more formidable orators of the twentieth century and a fine lawyer, recalled his pupil master saying to him, 'People pay us for our certainty, not for our doubts.'

6. **This is the theatre of the absurd** – something about standing up in public and talking has always (once I conquered my nerves) made me giggle. And in truth many presentations are absurd, especially in a world where jargon is rife. A few years ago someone invented 'bull-shit bingo' – a game in which you drew a square within which were 36 squares. Each square contained a piece of management jargon – going forward, strategic, focus, blue sky, global, scale-up, bench-marking, culture, ratio, downsizing, outsourcing and so on and so on. The game was to mark off each loathsome word as it occurred and if a vertical or horizontal line was filled then the lucky winner leapt to their feet shouting 'bullshit'. Avoid all jargon, speak English – in short sentences with short words. And remember that the way a script is written bears no relation to normal writing – it should have short sentences, big type; it should be fast . . . conversational . . . bold. The best speech writer I've encountered recently is Hilton Dawson, CEO of Shaftesbury Homes and the children's charity Arethusa. Ex-MP for Lancaster and Wyre, he is devoid of that posturing and Tupperware opaqueness that so many politicians have as stock in trade. Hilton speaks and writes simple man-in-the-street English – it's a refreshing change. They should probably have made him prime minister.

7. **Enjoy the drama** – you know where you are, why and to whom you are talking. You have a good, simple, strong story and the logic is sound and bombproof. The slides are coming along nicely. Yet you need to impart some surprise or 'oomph' into it at, say, two points

so that you stand out from your colleagues (in other words your competitors) and so that the audience remembers your key message. Vivid recollections of mine focus on disasters – the slide projector catching fire with the slides melting in front of us . . . 'why we shall succeed' dripping into the reproachful word 'succ' which slowly blackened and disappeared; the slides that had been fed in back to front making it look as though we were watching a presentation in an eastern European language. Think of what you most want your audience to remember and then brainstorm a solution that dramatises the point. It could be a huge word on the screen, a piece of animation or video or soundtrack, a great quote – or you could remove your jacket, tie and shoes saying 'this is about removing excess cost and baggage'. Whatever. It's about finding just one moment when you go for a bit of dramatic emphasis.

8. **Breathing life into your stuff** – on the road to brilliance you have to learn to make what you have to say attention grabbing and interesting. When you stand up there you have to look as though you care. You have to breathe life into the case you are making. You have to be a passionate salesman for your cause. You have to be (and be seen to be) really glad to be doing your presentation. I was recently at an event celebrating an Afruca anniversary (Africans Unite Against Child Abuse). While there, I reflected how much better the Africans were at demonstrating passion, sincerity and involvement. The reason, I suspect, that so few CEOs currently come from the UK is that we are pretty hopeless at being extrovert – unlike the South Africans, Zimbabweans, Australians, Americans, French, Italians. So when you get up there give it some 'welly'. Be animated – look and sound *dynamic*.

9. **Learn some Shakespeare and declaim** – could be Keats, Shelley, T.S. Eliot or Roger McGough – anyone you like. Just learn

it and then try saying it out loud – in the bathroom to start with, then outside. Raise your voice and let go with exaggerated theatricality. Enjoy yourself. All I want is for you to be in total control of content so that you can focus on delivery. For example, imagine reciting *Ode to a Nightingale* to a child, your parents, an old lady, someone dying, a lover, in a large church to 200 people, in a sitting room to 12 people. The exercise is in learning, delivering the same thing in different contexts and exploring your own range of expression. Enjoy!

10. **Practise, practise, practise** – you will need technical run-throughs and you will need to know your material well. Also the situation may be changing, which means you might have to be nimble-footed enough to change parts of your presentation at the last moment. But most of all you must leave yourself enough time to explore performance – to work on pace, on pauses, on the louder and on the softer bits. Don't imagine that any good performance you've ever seen wasn't very well practised. Practise alone so you get used to your own voice. Don't do what some have attempted – editing and moving material around while performing. This is nerve-racking for technicians and rotten for the performance – what you have when you start is what you go with. Do at least two trial runs – the first is what I'd call a 'walk-through', just to make sure all the elements sit together; then a 'run-through' which is a rehearsal with feeling. Mark up your script with cryptic notes and dream the performance in slow motion. Have a plan B – there could be a power cut or a fire, maybe hardly anyone turns up, maybe you are the only speaker standing because of dodgy pasta at dinner which you alone missed because you were rehearsing. There is no substitute for maximising your chance of success through practice.

A little bit of theatricality is vital on stage

You are not there to talk or to read a script – you are there to command attention and convince. Tom Peters and Jim Collins are engaged in current energetic debate about styles of leadership. The former advocates charismatic, nosy, female and iconoclastic; the latter is all for quiet, reserved, process driven, short term versus long term.

Well we don't have a 'long term' any more – we have *now*. And if you're on stage we have no place for the Quiet Man – remember the Ian Duncan Smith debacle? Aim for a powerful performance with lots of feeling and loads of confidence – plus.

> IF YOU'RE ON STAGE WE HAVE NO PLACE FOR THE QUIET MAN. AIM FOR A POWERFUL PERFORMANCE WITH LOTS OF FEELING AND LOADS OF CONFIDENCE – PLUS

9   I've got the power

PowerPoint is regarded as a critical tool by many presenters. Opinion about it is polarised – I regard it as a very useful tool that focuses thinking and enables you to produce, at the very least, easy-to-assimilate handouts and, at best, really swinging slides. Even so, it's just a tool. This chapter is more about process than anything else. But do remember that if you want the best from your career-shaping presentation then create a relationship with a professional slide designer and marvel at the difference – between your fast food and their cordon bleu.

PowerPoint

There are, we're told, 30,000,000 PowerPoint presentations done every day – or, if you prefer, 350 start every second of our lives. That's 1000 since I started typing this sentence (I'm a very slow typist). Around 11 billion presentations a year are hitting the population – that means there are about twice as many PowerPoint presentations a year as there are people on the planet. There are PowerPoint presentations everywhere.

Radical mind day and night all the time ... Maniac brainiac winning the game
'I've Got the Power', Snap

I love it because it is one of the newest persuasion tools around – it's certainly maniac and it can be 'brainiac' too.

It started in Silicon Valley in the late 1980s – a guy called Bob Gaskins, a Berkeley DPhil, had the idea. He developed it with Dennis

Austen at a small company called Forethought. PowerPoint 1 was first designed for Apple Macs in black and white, followed quickly by the colour version. This was followed by their being bought by Microsoft at the end of that same maniac year for $14 million. Bob must have thought 1987 was full of Christmases. I wonder what he thinks now.

PowerPoint has many strengths including:

- making people begin to think visually;
- great for consistency – leading to a coherent, corporate feel;
- it can create greater memorability of the piece as a whole.

However, it has weaknesses too:

- it is very easy to manipulate, which generally leads to too many charts;
- too much time is wasted on tweaking;
- presentations are generally ugly because people are not trained in design.

Be fair – blame the workman not his tools

The apparent weaknesses of PowerPoint are about misuse of the tool rather than anything being intrinsically wrong with the tool itself. It's like blaming the ballpoint pen for producing boring documents. You really can't blame PowerPoint for the bad thinking of those who jump in to use it.

> IT'S LIKE BLAMING THE BALLPOINT PEN FOR PRODUCING BORING DOCUMENTS

PowerPoint is easy to use, but very hard to use well. It's just like dancing – any fool can jive, but watch a professional do it. PowerPoint is like 'painting by numbers' – it gives the illusion of craftsmanship but in fact it just gets you on the road to painting. This is about allowing anyone and everyone to have a go. Anyway, for most people PowerPoint is the only useful and usable show in town so far as presentations go.

PowerPoint has improved lives

In the so-called 'good old days' we had art-worked slides that cost £20 each and took two days to prepare by experts. Or we had overhead transparencies, which are still a fine tool for small groups – you can even write on them.

When we moved to computer-generated graphics the first projectors took hours to set up – three guns, each of which needed to be put in focus – and were very sensitive, one knock and you were done for. They cost over £25,000, about the same as a concert grand piano. Now a superior digital product with a single lens as opposed to three, with auto-focus and auto correct for keystoning costs about £500, about the price of a reasonable electric guitar.

You click on PowerPoint and there they are – a series of some 30 templates. You choose one – there are only three or four that I find useful – you type in your presentation content and in about half an hour you have a half decent presentation – but it's in draft, only in draft at this stage. The dish is still raw.

You then put your slides into notes page format and work on simplifying the slide, above what is now suspiciously beginning to look just like your script. As with sauces you reduce and you reduce. You are an intelligent human being and this is just the beginning of a long iterative process.

Those who don't like it describe such presentations as 'death by PowerPoint'. However from a presenter's perspective it's 'life by PowerPoint' because the relatively PC illiterate among us can work, refine and improve all through the night without backup. We have been liberated.

Ten rules for doing your own slides

Assume you are busy, busy, busy and have to get this cracked quickly.

1. Don't get obsessed with the pictorial side of things or elaboration – focus on the story and the overview.

2. Set up your template by starting with the Slide Master so that your style – font, bullet points, indents and so on – is consistent. Make sure it looks like what you want to start with.

3. Write a contents page – this gives you a format, and a series of signposts all in the right order. This will vary from situation to situation but it helps the audience if they know that you know where you are going.

4. Always have a heading on your slide which says 'Strategy', 'Objectives', 'Challenges' or whatever but never more than 5–6 words – never. And always in lower case – it's easier to read.

5. Never use more than five bullets or 30 words a slide, except for handouts.

6. Leave gaps for pictures and diagrams which may come later.

7. You will always overwrite to start with so regard this as your handout.

8. Now fill in the gaps. Keep it all cryptic – your sort of words, avoid jargon, use simple visuals.

9. Now focus on refining and reducing your presentation – it is your musical accompaniment – there to make you look good and your meaning clear. It's there to tell your story.

10. If you have time then pass it to an expert to tidy it all up, and at least take out the ugly bits – better still, ask for a professional touch.

Let's get a bit more technical

Here are a series of simple things you need to do to stop you making stupid mistakes when making your own slides.

■ Do not use subheads and sub-bullets.

- Do not have complex charts – five simple ones rather than one complex one is preferable.

- Do not muck around with fonts and colour schemes – choose a simple scheme and stick to it.

- Ariel and Times Roman are pretty well foolproof – fonts like Tahoma may not be. If you insist on unusual fonts your lovely presentation may go awry with funny line breaks and half the text lost.

- Avoid animations, transitions and sound effects unless you have real expert backup.

- Do not type your script on screen and then read it out – pity the poor audience.

- Do not include elements that may not work on other computers – taking risks with technology is like accelerating on black ice, a recipe for ignominy.

- Do not assume that everyone has an up-to-date PC like you.

- Buy an up-to-date laptop which you will henceforth call the 'AudioVisual backup device'. Do not call it a computer – IT departments get funny about stuff in their territory. AV devices are usually someone else's problem but backup devices are absolutely fine, provided they don't impinge on the IT budget.

- Recognise that there is a difference between producing slides for projection in a big room and handouts for takeaway. The two are not the same, but many people assume they are.

Things to do to your PC

- Modify your toolbar so that it is easier to work with – half the stuff there you just don't need.

- Use the Slide Master, which you'll find under Master View – it enables you to store information about font, positioning for text and objects, bullet styles, background design and colour schemes to be applied to all your slides, including any you may add later. It also allows you to apply retrospective global changes – like changing font or colour – to all your slides.

■ Under Tools/Options/Save you'll find 'Allow fast saves' – turn it off because it inflates the size of the file, as well as making it more prone to corruption.

■ Use PowerPoint help groups (for example, http://office.microsoft.com) for tips and short cuts.

■ Find useful short cuts and keep a list of them – for example Shift F3 turns everything into capital letters, Ctrl B or I or U formats a highlighted section to bold, italic or underlined respectively.

■ Check your presentation prints in greyscale.

■ Watch news programmes to see how the real experts use and develop graphics – by studying weather presentations on BBC and ITV for example.

■ Most important of all, if you want to be competent with PowerPoint you have to practise, practise, practise.

■ Use the following websites to get advice, help and ideas:
   – www.showcase-online.co.uk
   – www.rdpslides.com/pptfaq

Having spent a significant part of my life in advertising, I do not believe it's worth bringing in professionals unless you brief them properly. If you are going to work well, with or without them, you need to apply the following rules.

Ten top tips on helping to create brilliant slides

1. **Practise PowerPoint** – how can you seriously expect to be any good at PowerPoint unless you constantly practise it? Those with real talent start with two things, an eye for design and a job – which means they do little else other than slides morning, noon and night.

2. **Exercise self-discipline** – I mentioned earlier the 'corporate porridge' imposed by corporate design templates. Well, unless you are CEO, stick to the rules and work within them. There are no prizes for being radical when radical is illegal.

3. **Work with experts** – learn new and different techniques by working with PowerPoint experts. At very little cost they will show you short cuts and effects you haven't properly understood before.

4. **Study design** – look at the BBC for instance – they don't use PowerPoint but they are usually good at design. So is the FT. So is the *Sun* – study how they make their audience focus. We are, as a bunch of business people, hopeless at design. Become a 'design junky' – it's one of the skills that we in the UK are still notable for.

5. **Use notes pages** – they help you to get that critical point of distinguishing between what you think *you* need to perform and what the audience needs to see.

6. **Fire the bullets** – try to do a presentation free of bullet points and see what happens – you might liberate yourself from the 'bam-bam-bam' effect they tend to have.

7. **The key is to find what you can't do** – if there is any really legitimate criticism of PowerPoint it's that it masks incompetence, not just from the audience but also from the presenter. You need to discover what you can and can't do if you are going to get better at it.

8. **Focus on the 'big one' to start with** – this is the Jack Welch thing which says you need a killer strategic slide – one which clarifies your message in a devastatingly clear way. Learning to use PowerPoint can help you to break your thoughts into logic-sized lumps. Thinking more positively about visuals in presentations can

▶

take you from average to excellent, or apprentice to brilliant, really quickly.

9. **Never confuse handouts with screen works** – yet everybody does. We live in a 12-inch world of laptops and when we come to present to a larger audience we sometimes can't understand why what looked great in Kew at 11.30 p.m. on your PC looks disappointingly dull in the Queen Elizabeth Hall the next day. Big is not beautiful – it's merely *bigger*. And the really bad thing about bigger is that it magnifies amateurism. What we produce for handouts and what we show on screen are not the same.

10. **Never use the word 'deck'** – this is the word made famous in the 1970s when IBM was more famous for its presentations than commercial success. Why does it worry me? It sounds big and heavy – as though you could stand on it. It also sounds violent – 'I'll deck you'. What it doesn't sound is fun.

One chance and only one

There is only one 'first night' when you do a presentation. You can't come back the next day having ironed out the wrinkles. You can change anything *now* – but you can change nothing afterwards (apart perhaps from your job). So practise now, as though your life depended on it. PowerPoint can liberate and enable you to visualise how to make a presentation work brilliantly.

But don't be an idiot by being a DIY bodger. You can do a small-scale presentation off your own bat but, however much you play with it, don't try doing a bigger performance without design professionals. If you do you'll regret it. After all you are the script writer and performer. Get the professionals to do set design, effects and stage management – under your direction, of course.

You thought the technical stuff was easy?

So you have a plan, a story – you even have some pretty good slides. What can go wrong?

- The venue is terrible with pillars that get in the way. You did check it yourself? Ah, you left that to an assistant. Hmmm!

- It's got a terrible accoustics – errible coustic…oost…ic… You did at least check this didn't you? You didn't! That was like buying a suit without checking the size and without trying it on first. Lunatic!

- The projectors are underpowered so your subtle coloured slides look washed out – a bit like you'll do by the time you've finished your show.

- You decided to present using a laptop screen to 20 people. Huge error – tiny screen, and irritated audience.

- Headline fonts should be 44 point or thereabouts and text should not go below 20 point. Hard-to-read charts are the first and worst cardinal sin. Bravely you ignore this and watch in dismay as all these myopic 50- and 60-year-olds walk into the room. Pity but they won't be able to read the slides at all. Are you in trouble!

Anyway, you're ready to roll – here are some reminders.

- Don't read the slides.

- Have cryptic notes on your notes page, which you use as your script guide.

- Writing good scripts is a *very, very* different art to writing an article, an e-mail or a book.

- Your script is there for you and no one else – so have it in huge print and short sentences.

- Avoid big slabs of text – you'll lose your place.

- The best presenters go through a five-stage process:
  - think
  - notes
  - script

- cryptic script
- notes.

■ Always write your own scripts – reading other people's is lazy and will consign you forever to being a boring novice.

■ Do not allow yourself to overrun – this is a crime equivalent to burglary because you are stealing the audience's time.

■ Pauses are good … long pauses can have a very dramatic effect. Important though the audience is, make it clear that you are in charge of this pause and that you haven't simply dried in blind terror. One speaker employed the dramatic pause too liberally and someone in the audience stood up and asked 'Are you all right?'

But most important of all are the following three things:

■ **Plan** so that you really know what you are trying to do.

■ **Rehearse** so that you leave nothing to chance. This does not mean going through your presentation so many times that even you get bored with it. It means knowing it well enough to know what comes next and to know where the high spots come.

■ **Spend twice as long** as you used to on preparing presentations and do as many as you can. It is only with constant practice that you'll really improve. Have you, for instance, ever heard of an accomplished linguist who spoke French, or whatever, only once a year? The harsh truth in life is that you have to work hard. As the great golfer Gary Player said, 'You know, the more I practise the luckier I get.'

However, it also makes great sense to regularly check out what you are doing right and not-so-right as a presenter. Do it with a professional, someone who is constantly exposed to different presenters. This will be refreshing and force exposure to the faults which in isolation may not be a big problem but which in combination may be holding you back.

I have a final and critical point to make – enjoy yourself! No, that's not a joke. But how you ask – how can you enjoy standing up there with shaking legs and the strong feeling that you now know what the onset of a heart attack feels like? Get used to being good – that's how. And when you've done a brilliant presentation, just the once, the euphoria will make you feel amazing and you'll find that you won't be able to wait for your next outing.

> DO IT WITH A PROFESSIONAL, SOMEONE WHO IS CONSTANTLY EXPOSED TO DIF-FERENT PRESENTERS

10 The book as a presentation

What follows is this book in PowerPoint. It shows how the use of PowerPoint is relatively easy to master. It also shows how good design can lift an OK presentation to something nearer music.

Following my own advice ... almost

I followed my own advice in reducing some of the key pieces of advice in this book into a 15-minute PowerPoint presentation – but I did it much too fast. There is a torrent of bullet points – a long stretch of sleeping policeman to destroy the axle of comprehension. And I have the design talent of a five-year-old.

Discovering what really happens

Creating a *basic* presentation is a breeze – brilliant it isn't but competent it is. PowerPoint, much derided by many, allows you to simplify your thoughts in a quite helpful way. What is here is a focus on *key thoughts* but the visual material is dull. At this stage this is just a good brief. Raw meat. Not a meal. Not yet.

I believe that brilliant presenting requires a balance of a whole bunch of elements, but that most of the time presenters are trying to avoid one or more of the following disasters:

■ dying on stage;
■ drying on stage;

- slides out of order, out of focus or just plain wrong;
- technical breakdowns – no mike, mike muffle or boom;
- an electrical blackout;
- a different audience to the one anticipated – 'no one said John Prescott was coming!';
- a *sudden* realisation that this is not an appropriate presentation for this particular audience.

Most of us are quite cautious when exposing ourselves to potential ridicule – rightly so. But being merely competent and having the chance to excel are not simple alternatives. Avoiding disasters and being brilliant are not bedfellows – one is defensive, the other aggressive.

> BEING MERELY COMPETENT AND HAVING THE CHANCE TO EXCEL ARE NOT SIMPLE ALTERNATIVES

Nearly all the potential disasters mentioned above are under your control, assuming you've got your nerves sorted out. Assume that you've done your homework – so you know about the coming of Mr Prescott. He's just a normal bloke with lots on his mind and a short attention span, but this is *your* show and the *audience's*, not his. Carry on and sock it to them, and if he is socked too then great.

The presentation that follows isn't inappropriate because it is descriptive and apolitical. The only time you'll encounter the inappropriate issue is in the over-bold use of risky humour, indiscretion and poor understanding of what is needed (read Chapter 4 again).

How to do brilliant presentations

The three presentations that follow are based on what this book is trying to achieve. There are three versions, starting with the basic

Version A. Version B shows what effect a little effort can have and Version C shows what a craftsman can do.

Version A

These are just notes at this stage – the shape of a story, a plot-line if you like. They might do for a handout. But the bones are there.

Planning is the key

Decide:-
- WHY are you doing it
- To WHOM are you doing it
- WHAT is your story
- HOW are you going to bring it alive
- WHERE is it happening
- HOW MUCH can you spend

Context

- What's going on in the world
- What's going on in the company
- What's going on with the brand
- What's going on with you
- What's going on with your audience

What's the story

- Key message
- The 'rule of three'
- Big start
- Bigger finish

- Checklist:
  - Simple
  - Less is more
  - Seize attention
  - Be memorable
  - Demand action

Getting in the colour

- Stories need descriptions
- Stories need anecdotes
- Stories need personal touches
- Stories need to be contemporary
- Stories need 'quotes'

Performing with power

- Control your nerves
  - breathe better
  - out of body confidence
- Be a bigger you
- Use your voice
- ACT – this is theatre
- Listen to the audience

  'Isn't it easier to act old boy?' (Sir Laurence Olivier)

Good slides will help

- Less is more
- But use more slides if this simplifies
- Slides are accelerators not brakes
- Don't look like everyone else
- Use your first draft as notes
- Get help to improve

Simple slides will help get attention.

Practice makes perfect

- **Plan**
  - what you say
  - the story line
  - the surprises
  - the context
  - the performance

- **Performance**
  - use pros to help
  - do run-throughs
  - simplify
  - rehearse
  - rehearse
  - get backup staff on your side

The stuff that gets forgotten

Before

- Agendas are like menus
- Things on seats set expectation
- Know your audience

After

- This is networking time
- E-mail presentation
- Keep their cards
- Answer their questions

How good are you?

1. Novice
2. Apprentice
3. Craftsman
4. Star
5. Brilliant

Getting better

Just three things:

1. Be honest about where you are now
2. Work on your material so you have a strong story
3. Practise like crazy

Summary

- Presentations can make you richer
- Plan how to get better
- Plan your next one better
- Spend more time on it
- Focus on: Context, Story, Colour, Slides, Performance, Before/After
- Work. Work. Work
- Get pros to help you

Version B

This shows the effect of a bit of a tidy-up but really not much more than that – it's a haircut not a makeover. An editor let loose on too many words.

Simplicity is a friend to comprehension. As you simplify your slides, making them more straightforward and with fewer bullet points, you should (I hope) see that your audience has a better chance of following you and the slide dancing together – as opposed to you doing a foxtrot and the slide doing the Gay Gordons.

This process takes time, just like cooking a sauce and reducing it to the perfect taste and consistency. This presentation is bubbling now but it still isn't cooked yet.

Better presentations
and how to do them

Richard Hall
August 2006

Presentations matter

You're on show
Opportunity to impact
Stir the audience
Educate!
Inspire!

Planning is key

Decide:
- WHY you are doing it
- WHO you are doing it to
- WHAT your story is
- HOW you will bring it alive
- WHERE it is happening
- HOW MUCH you can spend

Context

What's going on:
- in the world
- in the company
- with the brand
- with you
- with your audience

What's the story

- One big idea
- The 'rule of three'
- Big start
- Bigger finish

Checklist:
- Simple
- Less is more
- Seize attention
- Be memorable
- Demand action

Getting in the colour

Stories need:
- descriptions
- anecdotes
- personal touches
- relevance
- 'quotes'

Be a bigger you

Performing with power

- Use your nerves / breathe better
- Out of body confidence
- Use your voice
- Act – this is theatre
- Listen to the audience

Good slides help

- Less is more
- Break down complexity
- Slides are accelerators not brakes
- Be different
- Don't put your script on the slide
- Get the right support

Simple slides grab attention

Practice makes perfect

Plan
- What you say
- The story line
- The surprises
- The context
- The performance

Performance
- Use professionals to help
- Do run-throughs
- Simplify
- Rehearse
- Rehearse
- Get backup staff on side

The stuff that gets forgotten

Before

- Agendas are like menus
- Things on seats set expectations
- Know your audience

After

- This is networking time
- E-mail presentation
- Keep their cards
- Answer their questions

How good are you?

1 Novice

2 Apprentice

3 Craftsman

4 Star

5 Brilliant

Getting better

1 Be honest about where you are now

2 Work on your material so you have a strong story

3 Practise like crazy

Summary

- Presentations can make you richer
- Plan how to get better
- Plan your next one better
- Spend more time on it
- Focus on: context, story, colour, slides, performance, before/after
- Work – Work – Work
- Get professionals to help you

Version C

Enter the designer. The use of colour (use your imagination or check on my website, www.richardhall.biz) makes a big difference. Images, shape, drama – all these make a presentation better to look at and more fun to do.

Why the lemon? Being ironic and smart I could say 'to give it zest' because this is pretty well what it does. But I could also say 'to give it vitamin C' where 'C' stands for communication. It sets the literal message off in an appealing way.

Lemons, like presentations, are enigmatic things – they look like fruit and they smell fruity, but they are quite tart. They also give the presentation dimension and dynamic continuity. The lemon changes – it is not a logo – it goes through various recognisable conformations. It's an active not a passive lemon.

But this only the start of the design process to show the possibilities – we're beginning to see butterfly wings.

Better presentations
and how to do them

Richard Hall
August 2006

Presentations matter

You're on show!

Opportunity to impact!

Stir the audience!

Educate!

Inspire!

Planning is key

Decide

WHY you are doing it
WHO you are doing it to
WHAT your story is
HOW you will bring it alive
WHERE it is happening
HOW MUCH you can spend

Context

What's going on:

In the world
In the company
With the brand
With you
With your audience

What's the story

1 big idea	**Checklist:**
The "rule of three"	Simple
	Less is more
Big start	Seize attention
Bigger finish	Be memorable
	Demand action

Getting in the colour

Stories need:

Descriptions
Anecdotes
Personal touches
Relevance
"Quotes"

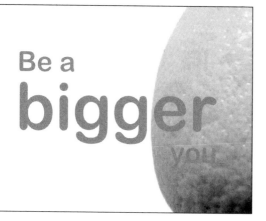

Be a
bigger
you

Performing with power

Use your nerves / breathe better
Out of body confidence
Use your voice
Act – this is theatre
Listen to the audience

Good slides help

Less is more
Break down complexity
Slides are accelerators not brakes
Be different
Don't put your script on the slide
Get the right support

Simple slides grab attention

Practice makes perfect

Plan	Performance
What you say	Use pros to help
The story line	Do run-throughs
The surprises	Simplify
The context	Rehearse
The performance	Rehearse
	Get back-up-staff on side

The stuff that gets forgotten

Before	After
Agendas are like menus	This is networking time
Things on seats set expectations	E-mail presentation
Know your audience	Keep their cards
	Answer their questions

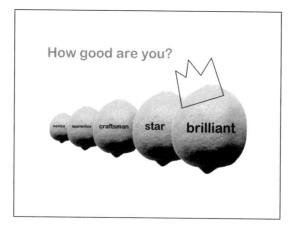

How good are you?

novice apprentice craftsman **star** **brilliant**

Getting better

Be honest about where you are now

Work on your material so you have a strong story

Practise like crazy

Summary

- Presentations can make you richer
- Plan how to get better
- Plan your next one better
- Spend more time on it
- Focus on: Context, Story, Colour, Slides, Performance, Before/After
- Work. Work. Work
- Get pros to help you

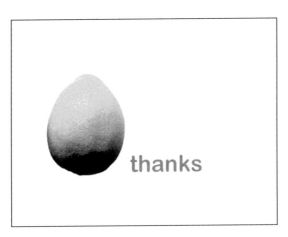

11 Really understanding your audience

You have all the talent in the world, have practised like crazy with a tight, solid story that is beautifully illustrated, and you can really understand the context in which you are appearing – and yet things can still go wrong. You have to do more – you have to really understand your audience.

What's up?

I recently heard the story about a well-known performer at conferences – known as a 'motivational speaker'. These are often terrifying people who have manic staring eyes and who speak very quickly using a lot of acronyms – 'TEAM – together everyone achieves more'. He arrived late – terrible traffic caused by an accident on the A1. Even Mr Motivational Cool was breathing a bit heavily as he rushed into the conference centre for the annual Spartemex conference. His contact from the company rushed up to him, 'Thank God you're here – we were so worried – you're on pretty well right away and they really need cheering up a bit – everyone's very down because . . .'. 'No time . . . sorry. I'm bursting for a pee and I need just two minutes alone to get my head together. See you by the stage.'

Two minutes later he sprang on stage giving big eye contact and bellowing 'Hello Spartemex – and how are we today?' Silence. Virtually everyone was looking down. 'Come on boys and girls get it together because you are a great team and you know what TEAM means – T...E...A...M , together everyone achieves more.' A girl in the front row stood up looked at him (at last a reaction) burst into tears and rushed off down the aisle howling. After half an hour he staggered off stage having tried everything and got no reaction apart from a series of people shaking their heads and walking out.

He spotted his Spartemex contact. 'What was all that about? That is the only disaster I've ever had and the worst audience I've ever come across.' His contact shook her head sadly. 'You were in such a state when you arrived that you didn't give me a chance to explain, and then you just pushed past me to get on stage. Our deputy chairman collapsed on stage in the middle of his speech of welcome and died. We all loved him. Everyone's feeling bereft.'

Mr Motivation had wondered about the ambulance that nearly drove him off the road as he made his hurried approach to the building.

Lessons on how to understand audiences

- **Lesson 1** – always make sure that you are totally and clearly briefed, especially on any areas of sensitivity. The new non-executive is Irish, no Irish jokes; the new CEO is a mathematician, no jokes at all; the deputy chairman has just died on stage, don't be jolly.

> MAKE SURE THAT THE SPEAKER IS TOTALLY AND CLEARLY BRIEFED, ESPECIALLY ON ANY AREAS OF SENSITIVITY

- **Lesson 2** – however hyped up you are, whatever process you use to get your adrenalin going, do not turn off your brain. Listen, look around you, understand.

- **Lesson 3** – know your audience. Who are they? What do they know? What do they want? Why are they here? What do they know about you?

- **Lesson 4** – when in doubt don't dig yourself into a hole. It's never stupid to actually get among the audience and see how they feel. And, by the way, never overestimate your ability to change the mood of a meeting.

- **Lesson 5** – not all, or indeed many, audiences are homogeneous. Understand all the undercurrents that exist. Do not present radical material to dyed-in-the-wool conservatives and expect applause. Don't invest your money on a potentially losing hand when you don't even understand the game you are playing. Get, or try to get, the audience on your side.

- **Lesson 6** – don't be boring. Get to the nub of what will 'sell'.

- **Lesson 7** – don't drink or carouse too soon before a presentation because it slows the brain.

Case study – a presentation to NBC Superchannel

No one had heard of it in the UK at the time. It now seems to be a cable channel. It's frankly rather confusing. Back in the mid 1990s I discovered one hotel – the Hyde Park as I recall – that was trialling it.

Being an energetic spirit I booked in, ate room service food, drank beer and watched the channel from 7.00 p.m. till 2.00 a.m. Now, I never watch much TV except when I have flu so this was a really strange experience. I watched people talking about their health – their legs, bowel movements and breathlessness – a session on share prices, some minor league baseball, a chat show with Jay Leno and, as I got sleepier, I seem to recall some soft porn.

In our straightforward presentation, in which boxes were being ticked or not, I had a slot in which to review the product and as time passed it seemed that I was probably the only person in the room (including those from NBC) who had an intimate and extensive experience of the product.

When I came to talk about it I must have taken leave of my senses. I extemporised and exaggerated about Jay Leno, about vitamin pills, about the business correspondent's cleavage ('the Dow's well down this evening . . .'). I even managed to make baseball sound funny.

▶

The guys and girls from NBC were in hysterics. My own team was laughing but in a slightly bemused 'follow that' sort of way. When it came to it, my contribution was funny but unfocused. Judge a presentation not by the applause but by the reviews – ours were not good and we did not win the business. Never let the performance devour the plot. Upstaging? Eat your heart out Brad Pitt. The NBC team left thanking me, ignoring the rest of the boring team (yes, they were very boring) and drying their eyes.

- **Lesson 8** – if you are presenting as a team then get it together. Never let one player go off dribbling the ball alone. Applause does not mean a good review. Pleasing people with your presentation is not the same as winning with it. You are there to win, not entertain.

- **Lesson 9** – listen to where your audience is and what they want. Indulge them, hit the hot buttons. And if you press a button and nothing happens then move on.

Overall then, you should not only know your audience but also feel their feelings, needs and hopes. You should respond to the vibes you get – and if you don't feel any then provoke some. You need to work with the audience's minds and develop what is going on in there.

> NOT ONLY KNOW YOUR AUDIENCE BUT ALSO FEEL THEIR FEELINGS, NEEDS AND HOPES

I am often asked to speak informally at weddings, funerals and other family events. The great thing about these is that their audiences are:

- full of politics – families always have undercurrents;

- replete with landmines – don't make any German, Irish, mother-in-law or whatever jokes (as if I would);

■ totally focused on the event in question;

■ friendly – willing you to succeed;

■ diverse in age and sensitivity;

■ waiting to be entertained.

I've had more fun and learned more about the pure art of presentation doing these than anything else I've ever done. Focusing on the subject and making sure that you romance, dramatise and make the subject look good is everything. Being upbeat and optimistic – even at funerals – is good. Not 'this is a catastrophic tragedy' so much as 'she died too young – of course – but look at all the great stuff she did while she was alive – and boy, was she alive.'

But most of all these occasions are about gauging the mood of, listening to, responding to and trying to achieve a real connection with the audience. They are also nerve-racking. 'I thought that strategic presentation was wrong – can we discuss the key elements?' is not what you ever want to hear, but the following is far worse, 'The family and I are very upset. I'm sorry but he was nothing like the man you described.' I have seen people create havoc at both funerals and weddings.

Given the opportunity to do any of the above speeches, celebratory or valedictory, do them. They are life-forming and you discover the core truths of presenting:

■ knowing your audience;

■ knowing your subject;

■ writing a great, positive essay;

■ simplifying it;

■ practising it;

■ using splashes of colour;

■ aiming to entertain;

■ listening and responding to your audience;

■ relaxing – they love you;

■ acting … this is not small talk – it's really big talk.

12 From ordinary to brilliant

By now you'll have made a few discoveries about yourself and about some of the techniques you need to employ to be brilliant. My guess is that you'll be discovering that you are doing better than you'd ever thought and that, with just a bit more effort, you could be even better. Don't worry because you are in good company. Until now presentation has not been in pole position, and it's time for a change.

A change and a commitment

I want you to make me a promise – on your next presentation I want you to triple the amount of time you spend on it. Before you get too far into it, I want you to score yourself on each of the following key elements on a scale 0–5, where 5 represents 'brilliant' in terms of where you'd normally expect to score and where, this time, you are determined to score:

- context
- story
- colour
- illustration
- performance.

Scoring anything over 18 will place you in the 'brilliance zone'.

You will discover that you will achieve an instant improvement just by focusing on this framework. But the real keys now lie with the content. If you know that you have a compelling story you will feel more confident and more inclined to go that extra mile. So I want you to spend a long time (through the night if needs be) on the content – the story and the colours you want to introduce into it.

Getting the story right will drive everything else

This is not going to be easy because you are probably straying into unfamiliar territory, where the idea of building a compelling story is alien to the way you normally work. I am asking for something that is:

- descriptive and vivid
- informative
- attention grabbing.

> THE IDEA OF BUILDING A COMPELLING STORY IS ALIEN TO THE WAY YOU NORMALLY WORK

And that requires a lot of hard work.

Take a piece of paper and start making notes – anything that comes into your brain. Circle words that seem as though they might make themes – growth, competitive pressure, innovation and so on – you know the kind of words around which others cluster.

It is here that brilliance has to kick in – the brilliance of making connections.

How do the superstars do it?

They generally apply four approaches that you will recognise when you see them at work. They may also work for you.

- **The power of intelligence** – the application of considered thinking. People like academics, senior civil servants or experts in their field use this to great effect.

- **The presenter as commentator** – this is where irony is used or where the speaker sees things from several points of view and comments on the different viewpoints. This is a common source of deadpan humour.

- **'I am very clever but I don't take myself too seriously'** – there is nothing better than seeing the big boss acting like a human being, or an expert speaking to non-experts at their level without being patronising. Not being too serious is a great way of getting very serious points across.

- **Deep knowledge lets you be very simple and very certain** – Simon Walker, of Reuters, talks of people who allude to something and appear to have pocketfuls of knowledge. It's always great to hear an expert talk their stuff, whether a sportsman or Bill Clinton. In your case talk about what you really know and it will have the same effect.

Ten top tips which take you into the brilliant zone

1. **Safety last** – when we do a presentation, all our instincts are to retreat into mediocrity. A 'brave presentation' has the same sound to it as the immortal 'courageous decision Minister' in the BBC series *Yes Minister* – decoded this means a rash and possibly career-damaging decision. Yet it is impossible to be a brilliant presenter if you only play safe.

   Rupert Howell, Chairman of McCann Erickson EMEA, has been known to sing at the start of a presentation. Bartholomew Sayle, who ran the Breakthrough Group, does the same to prove how far out on a limb he's prepared to put himself. I did it in a wedding speech recently. That's taking risks – if you heard my voice you'd

▶

realise this is very high risk. Who knows exactly what Seb Coe did at The London Olympic bid – but we can be sure that it wasn't ordinary.

My brother-in-law used to say 'boldness be my friend' before playing a slightly risky shot in golf – and, surprisingly, it often is.

2. **Steal brilliant ideas** – it was Picasso who said 'amateurs borrow, professionals steal' and if you want to be brilliant you must, above all, be professional. The other line I like is that if you borrow one thought it's called stealing, but if you borrow lots it's called research. So get your swag bag out and get stealing.

For a start, watch the best stand-up comedians and see how they work. Watch Jack Dee and see how he became 'king of laid back'. This happened because he failed as an enthusiastic comic – in the last few performances before finally jacking it in he stopped really trying and adopted the characteristic Jack 'sod-it' Dee mode. The audience response was ecstatic, and the rest is history. Watch my namesake Rich Hall for controlled anger and for going off on an amazing rant about accountants or whatever seizes his mind that night. Watch Jo Brand to see the mistress of measured exposition and irony. Watch Rowan Atkinson to see submerged mania threatening you and focused delivery where every word is like a sharpening knife. On a more serious note (not much more) watch Andrew Neill on *This Week in Westminster* to see a serious presentational tour de force by someone who uses every trick available.

Take every chance you can to see professionals at work then nick their best stuff, techniques and attitudes that seem to work for you – be shameless.

3. **Less is more** – as a simple rule, this alone will drive you to brilliance most compellingly. It was well recognised, not least by Mark

Twain, that it is harder to write good short pieces than good long pieces. The stream of consciousness is easy – sonnets or haiku are harder to write than ballads.

Reducing your presentation to its perfect state takes effort and time. Too many presentations are, as it were, undercooked – the sauce is thin and runny, the ingredients haven't blended together. When you are pulling your presentation together have a blue pencil beside you which is your 'brilliance editor'. I heard recently yet another great reason for cryptic charts from Ian Parker, one of the MDs at Royal Bank of Scotland Insurance – 'Do not trap yourself beneath a welter of words on a slide. How embarrassing to have "Growth is continuing to grow fast" when you have a sudden embarrassing hiccough. The single word "growth" allows you flexibility.' He's right. I suppose you could manage to say 'Growth has been great but can it continue? Look at last month – poor sales. Yet the underlying story is still good but you can take nothing for granted in the world today.' This, of course, is what modern management must have – the flexibility to respond to events as they occur.

Too many people inadvertently treat their presentations as suicide notes. Stories of the day before yesterday and worse … their ill-digested, uncooked ramblings on screen may help them keep on track but pity the poor audience. The next time you review a presentation that you are going to give make sure that you ask 'How can I reduce the stuff in here? How can I take words out of the slides? How can I achieve clear focus on the key issues?' Less is more is great advice.

4. **Being brilliant means being 'very something …'** – the danger lies in simple human nature – in wanting to disappear into the crowd. As our nerves get worse we want to hide under the blanket, sucking our thumb. But we need to be very brave to be very outstanding. Here are some of the options.

▶

- *Be very learned* – this works brilliantly if you are very learned and if you have the material to carry it off.

- *Be very funny* – this is all about risk and reward. Clint Eastwood as Dirty Harry said 'Do you feel lucky Punk? Well do you?' I feel much the same about humour in business.

- *Be very theatrical* – this can work brilliantly depending on the personality of the presenter and the nature of the audience.

- *Be very confident* – this will always work provided 'confident' doesn't become 'cocky'. Confident presenters calm an audience's fears and hostility; very confident presenters inspire them.

- *Be very smart* – it is brilliant to be presented to by someone who convinces you that they really understand what's going on in a consumer's mind. George Davis, creator of the very successful Per Una fashion range for Marks and Spencer, is totally convincing in his claim that he really, really understands women and what they want. He sounds very smart.

- *Be very cross* – I don't really recommend this unless you are Tom Peters who rants and raves and gets paid a fortune for doing it.

- *Be very enthusiastic* – far too many managers in business nowadays seem worn down by their bosses or by the rigours of the job to the point that they seem unenthusiastic. Enthusiasm in presentations can lift you into the 'brilliance zone' faster than anything else I can think of.

5. **Brilliance lies in pubs and shops, not at desks** – my point is totally serious. People working with other people will, on balance, be more likely to produce brilliant stuff than people flying solo. Brilliance is found outside yourself, not inside. What you do is provide the electricity that links the elements together. Tom Peters said 'No one ever wasted money travelling' and he's right, insofar as the brutal reality

of getting out from behind your desk and seeing new things can make you do and think more brilliantly. Heathrow will inspire you. It doesn't? It doesn't? Smack! Heathrow *will* inspire you – a vast city of transit and shops. Yes truly, all human life is there. It's a market researcher's delight. Spend time listening, looking, tasting, touching and smelling. You'll learn more about human nature in the perfumerie in Selfridges, Harvey Nichols or Harrods than you ever will in an office. You'll learn more having a good lunch with an engaging friend than you will reading *The Times* – which should anyway take only about 20 minutes, hopefully lunch will take longer. Brilliance comes from listening, absorbing and then recreating. Brilliance doesn't exist in an intellectual monastery or nunnery.

6. **'Yes you can . . .'** – brilliance will only come from pushing yourself and giving yourself new and terrifying challenges. A challenge which evokes 'I really honestly couldn't do that – just beyond me – honestly', but which when met lifts you to new heights. Someone I know really well has been singing in choirs for years, a soprano. She sang in churches and cathedrals round Britain. She was a solid number two rather than brilliant. And then something terrible happened – her voice 'went'. She visited a specialist fearing the worst of all diagnoses – would she see another Christmas? He peered calmly at her larynx and diagnosed that the bit that was supposed to close in the voice box was staying slightly open. 'You need exercises' he said and recommended a singing coach. Six months later she is singing louder, clearer and much more confidently. She's even doing solos. A while back she couldn't really do much, now she can do anything thrown at her from 'Oh no!' to 'Me sir! Me Sir!' in a few weeks – from croaking misery to brilliant.

The lesson to be learned is that you will find that you achieve brilliance quicker by working with great coaches.

7. **Trust in yourself** – as I was lining up to play a tee shot over a lake someone said to me 'Trust in your swing'. Only years after that inevitable splash did I really work out quite what lay behind this. If you don't believe in the equipment and talent you have then you are in a very bad place. Be the first to praise yourself – be the first to say how great the good bits were and be confident enough to criticise the poorer bits.

There is one piece of advice I want you to copy and put in your pocket if your quest to be a brilliant presenter is genuine – *You are a brilliant presenter. Be yourself. Be active. Be fun. But every presentation you do is a 'crunch'. So just do it freshly, enthusiastically and with rigour. You can be a brilliant presenter. Just feel brilliant.*

8. **Write yourself a letter** – this is an extension of what appears above and a tool with quite amazing impact. Brilliance can only happen in an environment where praise is bestowed. Apart from painters like Cezanne who had a rotten time in their life, most great artists and, by definition, most great performers require praise to deliver the goods. So help yourself. Write that letter – *'Dear Richard, I want you to know you were great yesterday – really inspiring and funny but, more to the point totally focused . . . it was great to be there . . . you were brilliant.'* Self-indulgent? Ridiculous? Unnecessary? No – not if it achieves the key aim of making you improve and become, hopefully, brilliant.

9. **Be in a good mood** – it's really hard being brilliant when you are grumpy. One of the reasons that so many politicians become less effective as they spend more time in office is that they get tired and worn down by intransigent issues. Basically they become fed up and their one-time brilliance is blunted. So the next time you start to prepare a presentation, and especially as you actually perform, think hard about how happy you are and how glad you are to be doing it.

10. **Be incurably curious** – the stuff of all brilliant presentations is the unusual, the surprising and the novel. It's also true that people who have a big appetite for life and an unquenchable interest in it are generally the most entertaining company. Great presenters describe things vividly with the excitement of someone seeing something for the first time. There's a childlike sense of curiosity and discovery – try to be like that. The best example I have of this was at the Hay-on-Wye book festival some three years ago. Germaine Greer was running a tutorial on Blake's poem *The Sick Rose*. It is eight lines long and she spent over an hour dissecting it. This was one of the best hours I've spent for a long time. This curvy and now mature Australian sat on a chair centre stage and talked quite fast and very intensely. She demonstrated fierce curiosity. She really wanted to know what the poem meant. She interrogated it, rained questions down on it and was a restless source of 'don't get it, don't know, don't know yet'. She wrestled with the words and pulled each one to the ground where she pummelled the meaning out of it. It was completely absorbing and totally brilliant.

13 The graduation to brilliance

Relax. You've attained brilliance. People look at you in awe. They think you should become an actor. But you remain paranoid, frail and lacking in self-confidence. It doesn't get easier – you work harder, you get better and you know more of the tricks to get you by. But pay attention – this is theatre and it's different with every performance. That's what makes it fun as well as dangerous.

A scale of improvement

Let us suppose that you've done a lot of presenting and that you have become quite accomplished. When someone uses the 'P word' nowadays you don't feel a frisson of terror or hear the *Psycho* music. You just know it's 'presentation time' not 'shower curtain time' and that everything is all right.

You've stopped using the word 'presentation' though and just to help you and those around you to define the scale of an event you talk about:

- conversation
- talk
- gig
- show.

Everyone knows that 'show' involves the whole kit and will be full of appropriate effects and surprises – although the art of keeping surprises to a minimum is what characterises all the analysts' presentations anyone gets involved with.

Brilliant presenters, like you've become, are also pragmatists. Not every performance can be as brilliant as you'd wish, not every innings is a century, not every round is a 65, not every meal is Michelin 3*, not every day is cloudless. In the real world, and this is what makes live performance so utterly thrilling, there is variation in product. The story will be more, or less, convincing. The performer will be less, or more, on song.

> NOT EVERY PERFORMANCE CAN BE AS BRILLIANT AS YOU'D WISH, NOT EVERY INNINGS IS A CENTURY

However one thing will be absolutely constant and that will be your enthusiasm to improve. The better you get, the more self-critical you will become and the more time you will spend on trying to lift your game. Here, finally, are the key issues for brilliant presenters about presenting.

Ten things that even brilliant presenters have to remember

1. **Controlling nerves** – Mark Twain said 'There are two types of speakers, those that are nervous and those that are liars'. Even the best get butterflies and sometimes they get a shock. Like a sudden urge to do a runner, or a completely new sensation like trembling or the desire to go and have a pee. Tony Jeary has written a book *Inspire Any Audience* in which he confesses – and you've got to understand that, nauseatingly, he's called 'Mr. Presentation' – 'I'm always nervous before a presentation; the day I'm not nervous is the day I quit presenting.'

   I've discussed controlling nerves earlier. Having got to this stage of accomplishment it is very unlikely that you're going to be scared speechless but you will get butterflies – on checking, the collective is a 'rainbow of butterflies'. I rather like the thought of going on stage with a rainbow of butterflies coursing through one's veins. That sounds exciting but I also found another collective which describes brilliantly what it's like when you don't feel so good – 'a rabble of butterflies'. Those we can do without – go for rainbow not rabble.

For all you brilliants this is a management exercise. You must remain bodily and mentally self-aware, so those signals your body gives – 'I'm not feeling great, I feel a bit sick; I've got a headache; I feel lethargic' – are dealt with and placed under control with a dictatorial self-rebuke 'Feel like that later – not now.' In presenting, feeling in control is the key to delivering well. I call this 'taming the butterflies'.

2. **Enthusiasm sells** – overflow with it. Occasionally you have to deliver bad news to people but the roots of motivation lie in inspiring them. And there's too little of that happening right now. I think all cynics should be swiftly and mercilessly put out of their misery to prevent anyone suffering from further unconstructive gloom. Brilliant people can usually explain bad news well and offer the prospect of good news if certain courses of action are followed. Lady Thatcher used to say of Lord Young – then just plain David – 'Other people bring me problems; David brings me solutions.'

Brilliant people or communicators are seldom just cockeyed optimists but they always, in my experience, exude the belief that there is a solution even if it will take an effort to achieve it. Intriguingly, James Lovelock, author of *The Revenge of Gaia*, finds it possible to juxtapose the thoughts that 'As far as global warming is concerned the game is over' with 'but as far as individual countries are concerned, by focusing on solutions rather than global rhetoric, I am

▶

very optimistic' – particularly so of Holland and the UK it seems. Like it or not, audiences seldom respond to or remember presentational whackings.

We remember speeches like Harold Wilson's first as party leader when he talked about the thrill of technological advance and said 'This party is a moral crusade or it is nothing'. They liked David Cameron when he spoke – no, presented – at the Conservative Party conference and became the new leader because he spoke to their hopes for a new future and – good presentation trick – because he spoke without notes. This meant he really delivered his message from his inner being – it was belief not a speech.

3. **A funny thing happened on the way to the presentation** – humour, like adrenalin, is dangerous stuff in presenting – too much and you can lose your audience completely and for good. No one likes a second-rate comedian and the art of joke-telling to a few people, let alone a roomful, is highly specialised. Tommy Cooper had the ability, like Helge Fisher, the renowned Pilates teacher, who advocates the need 'to be' on stage a long time before you begin to think of 'saying'. He'd simply stand there, shrug and laugh and the whole of the Palladium would be in stitches. The only brilliant presenters I've seen who have a great feel for humour are Tony O'Reilly and Richard Eyres. The rest avoid the joke – they believe the risk is much higher than potential reward – but every brilliant presenter tells a great colourful story with ironic asides. On balance going for smiles and chuckles rather than belly laughs is the way forward. And remember how the audience feels – no one wants Mr. Grumpy. Good nature and good humour are powerful tools.

4. **On the magic art of delegation** – the mark of the most senior brilliant presenters is they will have a reliable team of professionals around them, certainly for all their major gigs and shows. These will

comprise a team to make the slides look great and work properly, a mentor to help ensure the material sounds good and that the story is communicating powerfully, people in charge of sound, lights, stage and so on, and a PA who has an even better memory than them. They will know all these people – they don't risk using untried hired guns – and these people know them. Hopefully, they also enjoy working with each other.

Most of us have less room for manoeuvre and smaller budgets at our disposal. You will – if you are smart – be doing a small amount of work with a professional communications expert and a slide producer to simply lift your game. DIY PowerPoint is very easy to spot and marks you out as a hands-on maverick. In 'conversations' and 'talks' that's fine – in bigger events it's frankly a little disappointing, as anyone who has done this will probably know to their cost. Brilliant presenters always know when to ask for help.

5. **The voice is the key to it all** – at any rate it is key to performance. There are some really talented voice coaches around. I've worked with the brilliant Suzi Grant, the ex-Channel 4, Sky TV presenter and now a best-selling author on diet. Her technique can best be described as the energetic and friendly pummelling of a victim until, viewing themselves on video, they start to project, to deepen and to pace their delivery. What she does to brilliant presenters is to make them act with their voices, use them as instruments. Her own voice is deep, throaty and rich with laughter – Fenella Fielding meets Mariella Frostrup.

Although I haven't yet worked with them, I've heard good things about Angie Konrad of Voicewaves and Chris Hughes Prior of Speech-Works *Plus*. Chris asks people if they sound 'rushed, lightweight or strained'. To which I imagine them squeaking 'What me? Not at all – erm – no, no not lightweight, Ha! Ha!' She and a wide range of voice trainers across the world are transforming people's job prospects because ironically they sound much more convincing although performance in their jobs may not be immediately improving.

However brilliant you are and have been, don't neglect the presenter's number one tool – the voice. Every so often go for a check-up – that's if you're going to do a lot of presentations and are going to stay brilliant at doing them.

6. **What is Your Voice? Who are You?** When James Wilde, the deposed CEO of Rentokil, said in indignation in his dying days 'I am a CEO, not an actor' he was right in one sense. Actors, like slide makers, give their all to their craft and are focused professionals. No doubt Terence Stamp would have delivered James' speech with more conviction but he would almost certainly have been a worse CEO. Yet you have to act. You may even have to lie or, at best, prevaricate. You may have to look upbeat when you know your new white hope drug is failing in tests. Honesty is not always the best policy. Timing how and when to break the bad news calls for the skill of an actor.

So decide what you are comfortable about:

- *how you sound* – I've advocated voice training. You need it, whoever you are, but you need to be the designer of this voice and have a strong sense of how *you* want it to sound and develop.

- *who you are* – or rephrased, how you are perceived. For example Sir Michael Edwardes, one of the most admired businessmen of our generation – small, powerful, punchy, competitive, South African, totally fearless. For example Stelios Haji-Ioannou, founder of EasyJet speaking at Reuters – a big man, he stands up and prowls around, describes his empire brilliantly and as a presenter has great lines. When asked 'What advice would you give to any budding entrepreneurs?' he answers 'Have a rich father. Next question.' At this 'brilliant level' you need little help other than to check and recheck that you are keeping up to the mark.

The world still makes superficial judgements – recognise this rather than resent it.

7. **Brilliant presentations challenge convention** – *The World is Flat* is the name of Thomas Friedman's book. It's a great title. It is counter-intuitive in the same way that Edward de Bono's *I am Right and You are Wrong* is, but in the latter instance I have a horrible suspicion that the author actually thought that he *was* right and that we *were* wrong, and that he wasn't being ironic at all. Is that true Edward? No. So I am wrong. And you are right.

Brilliance comes frequently – not always in surprising people. Christopher Ricks, Professor of the Humanities at Boston University and Oxford Professor of Poetry, is a passionate fan of Bob Dylan and argues that *Lay Lady Lay* is from the same blood line as John Donne's love poetry 'Come madam, come, all rest my powers defy until I labour, I in labour lie'. I love the thinking that at one and the same time places Donne in a contemporary context and Dylan in a timeless one. Ricks says it so simply and so brilliantly – he really has the true presenter's touch when he says 'Great minds think and feel alike'. If you aspire to brilliance you must be able to make connections like this increasingly often.

Brilliant presentations change things, and things are changed by an audience being engaged and being persuaded to think and to see things differently. Read the clearest thinkers around who try to change minds – Friedman, Ricks, Matthew Parris (on his day), Malcolm Gladwell, Tom Wolfe (still), Anatole Kaletsky, Lucy Kellaway

▶

and so on. In a world changing as fast and dramatically as ours, brilliance in presentation is unlikely to come from conventional been-there-seen-that thinking. The world really is flat.

8. **Have I Got News for You?** This incredibly popular BBC TV series found its inspiration in the current news and the apparent improvisation genius of the key players. Some of this, it turns out, is pre-planned – so there goes another Santa Claus legend, deflated and debunked – but some of it is clearly live and for real and very, very funny. We can learn two things from this – be in touch with the events of the day, anything that might be relevant to your presentation, and what the headlines are elsewhere in the world. For instance, just look at www.wnsociety.com and you're living in the global economy. Find the funniest off-the-wall stories – Victor Lewis Smith in *Private Eye*, the *Financial Times* for the occasional blinding insight, and *The Week*. To learn about China visit www.danwei.org for some brilliant stuff; for wonderful American lunacy www.theonion.com does it; for great solid management stuff try http://fastcompany.com; for innovation and funky new ideas www.springwise.com. Brilliance does not come in a room. It comes from walking the street, the stores, talking to people, reading, making connections and, critically, from being prepared to push yourself to think the unthinkable.

If you're going to be brilliant, as I've said before, use the best help you can find – global thinkers, intriguing writers, batty eccentrics – anyone or anything that gets your brain going. Brilliance has opinion – have a few themes that people could get you going on and which could fill a rant of an hour or more. For me these would currently be China, bullying in the workplace, ensuring that all employees are taught the art of presentation, momentum marketing, the future and how this impacts on *you*, and why guerrillas always win. Choose your own and have a few 'off the peg' presentations – things you feel strongly about that you can keep up to date with new examples and stories.

Brilliance is rarely extempore, it is almost always based on rigorous knowledge, but if you have one of a series of 'passion subjects' to hand and are willing to take the risk then you can run a question and answer session and an 'apparently' improvised show that will amaze people.

9. **The audience is right** – as the president of Orvis once put it, 'The consumer's right even when they are goddamned wrong.' In my experience audiences, on balance, would prefer an agreeable to a boring or dispiriting time. One of the best presentations I did was with Chris Pinnington of Euro RSCG. It was a pitch for a firework safety campaign by the DTI to Baronness Denton. We kept it really short – maybe ten slides, lots of space for questions and answers. She was preoccupied in the tiny room we had to present in at Millbank House opposite the House of Commons and she was con-stantly looking at the TV screen. People complained that she was being ill-mannered and not paying attention – then we realised that she was speaking in a debate later and was fitting this in. We won. We got our audience dead right. We were also very good.

10. **When it all goes wrong** – there are no guarantees. You've researched the venue, prepared the piece, you've got a great story and stunning slides with the best backup team in London who, playing safe, even have two computers. What could go wrong? Wow – use your imagination:

- a terrorist attack
- a tube strike
- a flood

▶

- a strike in your own company

- a product recall – remember the £20 million Cadbury cover-up?

- you have laryngitis, flu or a major stomach upset

- your deputy chairman dies

- a consumer dies from eating your product

- a power cut

- a moment of insanity from one of your backup team

- the police arrive just as you are about to start and arrest your stage manager for non-appearance at court on a trivial driving offence.

Nearly all the disasters I've met have been turned into great triumphs by brilliant presenters in flashes of inspiration:

- they sit down and tell the whole unvarnished story;

- they turn it all into a questions and answer session;

- they get ice creams in for those who want them;

- they take charge in a totally different way breaking the audience up into small groups and running on-the-spot focus groups.

The real brilliance is in managing situations so you achieve solutions that are effective and memorable. I have assumed that you are brilliant, and therefore that you will be respected for what you can do and achieve. What you will do – being brilliant – is avoid taking anything for granted.

THE REAL BRILLIANCE IS IN MANAGING SITUATIONS SO YOU ACHIEVE SOLUTIONS THAT ARE EFFECTIVE AND MEMORABLE

The final thing is that brilliance depends on having brilliant people as mentors and advisors – people who can help you to turn an ordinary presentation into a memorable or even a brilliant one.

14 So you've made it

But can you remember how to do it time after time? I strongly recommend that you read this final chapter before every presentation you do, however brilliant you are. Read it again and again. It'll stop you making sloppy mistakes or falling back into bad habits.

This is a formula

There's nothing magic about any of this, just the need to listen to the professionals. Follow the 'brilliant presentation' format and work really hard at it. The idea of a quick fix is appealing but is as misguided as a crash diet:

- You need practice to get good.
- You need to be honest about how good or bad you are to start with.
- You need to devote more time to planning, writing and rehearsing than you could imagine possible.

The biggest change that you'll notice is that you will begin to *want* to present and, however much you may protest, a certain thrill will fire in your stomach as opposed to a dread of anticipation. If you've read this book and are prepared to devote time to improvement then it is unlikely that you won't have improved massively already.

> A CERTAIN THRILL WILL FIRE IN YOUR STOMACH AS OPPOSED TO A DREAD OF ANTICIPATION

This is a very competitive world and there are many very young people who find the act of standing up in front of their peers is a lot less alien than it used to be. People are judged by how they perform in public because it shows:

- how confident they are in their own ability;
- the potential of the business they represent;
- how well prepared they are;
- how knowledgeable they are;
- how attuned they are to their stakeholders;
- how inspirational they are as leaders;
- how responsive and flexible they seem to be;
- how with it they are.

How with it are you?

In a world shaking up and shaking down as much as ours, a world in which the 'American dream' declines in the face of the 'Asian explosion', we'd better have a global viewpoint and a sense of why what the *Economist* mischievously called 'Chindia' is so important. These are not just 'emerging economies', they are the future of the world.

Our ability to deal with the new icon of the twenty-first century, St. Paradox, and communicate the challenges that exist to those around us in a clear and inspiring way will be what distinguishes the successful from the average executive.

Presentation has never been more important

In business, brilliant presentation to our stakeholders – workforce, peers, competitors, customers, consumers, suppliers, investors, media, analysts, business experts and opinion formers – has never been so important. Brilliant presentation comes, more than anything else, from clarity of thinking and empathy with the audience, and the clear thinking and understanding that will give us the best chance of building a better world.

The tools of the discipline have been described already – but, as any brilliant presenter will tell you, repetition does not go amiss.

- **Decide how good or bad you are** – analyse your strengths and weaknesses. Given how important the art and craft of presentation are, do not try to hide or wriggle away from your shortcomings. Talk to others if you think you are already perfect – their comments may be helpful. Get a fix on where you stand and what a reasonable target is. This is about planning your future, not hoping for the best.

- **The context** – spend as long as it takes before you ever start thinking about what you are going to say and how you are going to say it. Work out *why* you are doing the presentation, to *whom*, how they *feel* and what they *think*, *what's* going on around them, *where* you are doing it, *how many* will be there. Leave nothing to chance – be very clear about the context in which you are performing. Get your understanding of context wrong and the rest will unravel.

- **The story** – the key message, the central big idea. How does it develop? How can you tell it clearly and compellingly? Do you have the 'elevator pitch' or synopsis of the plot absolutely clear – so were someone to say 'Richard you have only two minutes to do your presentation to us, not half an hour' could you do it? Become a great storyteller and you could become a great leader – it's that simple.

- **The splashes of colour** – the stuff that enlivens, dramatises and makes it exciting. The bits of contemporary fact, the anecdotes, the data, the evidence that makes the story completely unforgettable and convincing. These are the spear carriers, the crowds, the extras, the props that make the story more fun. Remember *The Winter's Tale*, 'Exit pursued by a bear' – great stage direction, great fun. But it's more than fun – character and intelligence add colour and memorability to a show.

- **The visual backup** – the slides, the staging, the 'toys' you use to make a memorable point. These are there to enhance but never to run the show. Make sure they are good enough to not hamper the rest. Learn to do your own by all means but take professional advice when it comes to a big show so that you are up with or ahead of other speakers. Good slides speed you up, make you feel good and keep the audience on your side without demanding too much of them.

> DO YOUR OWN BY ALL MEANS BUT TAKE PROFESSIONAL ADVICE WHEN IT COMES TO A BIG SHOW

- **The performance** – a nerveless tour de force is what you should be aiming at. Control your butterflies, make sure you are in good voice, use coaches to transform you from being apologetic (very bad) into a good-humoured energy source (very good). You are on stage – act like you own the space, the story and, for so long as you are up there, the attention of the audience. Have fun – this is not a board meeting, this is theatre.
- **Being in control** – you are a control freak or, better still, you are surrounded by control freaks who will leave nothing to chance. You have created a brilliantly unusual agenda and you have great take-aways. You are thinking of new ways to break the 'me up there and you down here' paradigm. This is your show – go for it. Before, during and after. This audience is yours forever.

Brilliance will be achieved if ...

- ... you decide you really want to enjoy presenting, not just to go through the motions.
- ... you believe you can, and then you succeed in controlling your nerves.

- ... you believe life is exciting and you have an avid curiosity about everything you read and see.

- ... you listen as well as you talk.

- ... you want to be great.

- ... you realise what others can do better, and use this when it matters.

- ... you practice.

While I can give you techniques to succeed, I can't give you that desire to excel. But if your desire to be brilliant is really obsessive then I think you are going to find that you like presenting a lot pretty soon.

Welcome to the theatre of presentation.

Index

ability, levels of 16–22
acoustics 75
acting 57, 60, 83, 88, 94, 103, 115
adrenaline 8–9, 16
agenda 24, 28, 42–3, 84, 90, 95, 130
alcohol 12–13, 101
anecdotes 33, 83, 88, 93, 129
appearance, personal 61–2
apprentice presenter 17–18, 85, 90
approaches to presenting 106–7
audience 11, 17, 21, 123
    characteristics 24–5
    involvement 44
    knowing your 84, 90, 95, 100
    listening to 83, 88, 94
    mood of 28–9, 102, 103
    size 25–6
    toys for 50, 130
    understanding 99–103
    vibes from 102
audio visuals 47–55, 130
    killer slide 42, 43–4
    number of slides 49
    professional help 48
    ten top tips 49–53
    see also PowerPoint

backup support 84, 89, 95, 118–19
bad news 117, 120
boring, avoiding being 55, 101
breathing 6, 8, 10, 13, 83, 88, 94
brilliance 21–2, 85, 90
    feeling brilliant 112
    five critical processes 3
    four key elements 21–2
    ten points for 107–13

bullet points 48, 70, 71, 73, 86
business cards 43, 84, 90, 95

catering 29–30
challenges, meeting 111
charts, killer 42
checklist, scoring yourself 105
coaching 9, 111, 130
    voice 61, 119–20
colour, adding 3, 39–46, 83, 88, 93, 103, 129
    top tips 40–4
comfortable, feeling 11
company requirements 19, 24
confidence 6, 11
connections, making 106, 121
context 3, 23–30, 82, 87, 93, 129
conventions, challenging 121–2
corporate templates 50, 73
craftsmen presenter 18–19, 85, 90
creativity 36, 45
curiosity 41–2, 113, 131

delegation 118
design process 91
disasters 79–80, 99–100, 123–4
drinking water 6

enthusiasm 2, 110, 117–18
exercises 10–13, 64–5
externalising 11

facts 1, 3
Financial Times 40, 41, 73, 123
FIRES approach 1–3
five critical processes 3
fonts 49, 50, 70, 71, 75
formula for brilliance 127, 130–1
freezing, avoiding 6–7
freshness 1–2, 22, 32, 45

handouts 70, 74
honesty about ability xi, 7–8, 85, 90, 127, 129
humour 80, 118

ideas book 42
importance of presentation 81, 128–9
improving performance 105–13
information, providing new 2

jargon 31–2, 63, 70

knowledge 21, 107

language, simple 20, 21
less is more 39, 93, 108–9
    slides 83, 89, 94, 109
levels of mastery 15–22
listening 131
    out and about 110–11
logical arguments 58–60

management books 40–1
managing situations 124–5
mission statements 2–3, 31–2
mood of audience 28–9
mood of presenter 112

nerves xii, 5–14, 29, 83, 88, 94, 109
    controlling 10–13, 116–17, 130
    exercises for 10–13
    symptoms 8–9
networking 84, 90, 95
news, using current 27–8, 40, 123
novice presenter 16–17, 85, 90
nude practice 11

off the peg presentations 122–3

passion 21, 64
pauses 76
performance 3, 52, 57–66, 83, 88, 94, 130
    dramatic emphasis 63–4
    killer moment 43–4
    stage presence 62
    ten top tips 60–6
Peters, Tom 21, 37, 41, 66, 110

Plan B 65
planning 11, 76, 82, 87, 92, 127, 129
    checklist 24–30
    practice 84, 89, 95
    to improve 85, 91, 96
posture 6, 62
PowerPoint 67–74
    examples 81–97
    strengths and weaknesses 68, 69
    using 70, 71–2
practice xi, 65, 85, 90, 96, 127, 131
    performance 84, 89, 95
    with PowerPoint 72, 74
    story test 35
praising yourself 112
preparation 12, 18–19, 58, 76
professional help 26, 76, 77, 84, 85, 89, 91, 95, 96
    audio visuals 48
    coaches 111
    PowerPoint 73, 74

quotes 41, 83, 88, 93

rehearsing 26, 65, 76, 84, 89, 95, 127
relaxation 6
relevance 2
risk taking 107–8
run-throughs 65, 84, 89, 95

script 6, 18, 75–6
self-awareness 7–8, 9–10, 117, 127, 129
self-belief 62–3
sensitive areas 100
seratonin 8–9, 16
singing for nerves 10
size of event 25–6, 49, 115, 129
slides 17, 20, 51, 83, 84, 89, 130
    bad 47–8, 53–4
    killer slide 18, 73
    less is more 83, 89, 94, 109
    rules for 55, 69–70, 83, 84
    simplicity 84, 89, 95
    words per slide 52, 70

small groups 16, 17
star presenter 20–1, 85, 90
stealing ideas 108
story 2–3, 21, 93, 103, 129
   adding colour 39–46
   freshness of 22
   inspirational 34
   rule of three 82, 87, 93
   top tips 32–3
   writing a great 31–8, 106
style 50, 109–10
   and voice 120–1
subject of presentation 23–4

takeaways 43, 130
team, working with 21, 118–19
technology 69, 71, 75
theatricality 52, 130
toys for audience 50, 130
trial runs 65, 84, 89, 95
trusting yourself 112
truth in story creation 33–4

up-to-date material 26–7

venue 28, 75
visual aids 3, 18, 130
   and size of group 26
   see also audio visual; PowerPoint
voice 5, 6, 7, 13, 50, 83, 88, 94
   coaching 61, 119–20
   and style 120–1

warming-up 6
Welch, Jack 3, 41, 42
wow factor 43–4, 46, 50